To K & B

About the Author

Lucy Kellaway is an English writer and teacher. For over twenty years, she was an observer of the peculiarities of corporate culture in her column for the *Financial Times*, before retraining as a teacher. She is a co-founder of the educational charity Now Teach and lives in London.

Praise for *Re-educated*

'There are lots of reasons to read this book, which has the fineness of detail, sharpness of humour and grace of a novel by Penelope Lively. But it's this business of changing one's mind – the thing most of us least like to do – that I admired the most' *Observer*

'Inspiring, insightful and sometimes sharply funny . . . In all her brave uncertainty, it leaves you sure of one thing: if the question is "Why start again in middle age?", the answer is a resounding "Why not?"' *The Times*

'A beautifully told story of courage, determination and, above all, magnificent defiance' *Alan Johnson*

'Bracing and inspirational' *Nigella Lawson*

'Candid, original, humorous, and sad. Lucy Kellaway has always been a wonderful writer. This is a life-affirming account of how and why she ticks' *Jon Snow*

'Funny and engaging' *Sunday Times*

'Dazzling . . . this wonderful, funny book is a celebration of the power of education' *Daily Mail*

'She writes with warmth, wit and honesty, turning her real life experiences of teaching in a Hackney school into what I hope will become a serious debate about what education is for' *Financial Times*

Re-educated

Why it's never

too late

to change

your life

Lucy Kellaway

EBURY
PRESS

1

Ebury Press, an imprint of Ebury Publishing,
20 Vauxhall Bridge Road,
London SW1V 2SA

Ebury Press is part of the Penguin Random House group of companies
whose addresses can be found at global.penguinrandomhouse.com

Penguin
Random House
UK

This book is a work of non-fiction based on the life, experiences and
recollections of the author. In some cases names of people, places
and the detail of events have been changed to protect the privacy of others.

First published by Ebury Press in 2021
This edition published by Ebury Press in 2022

www.penguin.co.uk

A CIP catalogue record for this book is available from the British Library

ISBN 9781529108019

Printed and bound in Great Britain by Clays Ltd, Elcograf S.p.A.

The authorised representative in the EEA is Penguin Random House Ireland,
Morrison Chambers, 32 Nassau Street, Dublin D02 YH68

Penguin Random House is committed to a sustainable future
for our business, our readers and our planet. This book is made
from Forest Stewardship Council® certified paper.

MIX
Paper from
responsible sources
FSC
www.fsc.org   FSC® C018179

Let God Laugh at
My Plans

Six years ago, I was living in a large, terraced family house in Highbury with a husband and four children. My life was a model of stability. I had been married to the same man for 25 years. For 15 I had lived in the same place, which itself was less than three miles from the large, terraced family house near Kentish Town where I grew up. I had worked at the same newspaper for 32 years, and every Monday for over two decades had written the same column.

Most mornings at 9.30am I would leave home on my bicycle and cycle through Clerkenwell and past St Paul's to the *Financial Times*, where an office full of hacks, many of whom had also been there for decades, sat at their desks drinking coffee out of cardboard cups. At the end of the day, I would get back on my bike and cycle home, where most nights I would set to and make supper for my children, my husband and for my dad, who lived nearby.

In the space of two years I tore it all down. House, marriage, job, considerable income – I dispatched the lot of them. And if that wasn't enough change to be getting on with, one May morning in 2016, Dad was dispatched from his own life – and from mine.

Now I live in a modern house in Hackney, sometimes alone; sometimes a changing selection of adult children live with me. Most mornings I leave home on foot at 6.45am, bound for the local secondary school where I teach economics to recalcitrant teenagers. I walk through the empty playground, brew some PG Tips in a dirty mug and head to my classroom for last-minute lesson planning before the school gates open at 8am. I earn a small fraction of what I used to. I get up earlier. I work harder. But I like my new life: it is right for me now, just as my old life was right for me then.

Shortly after my 60th birthday I told my sister Kate I was thinking of writing a book about having changed my life at the eleventh hour. It would be for all those people of a similarly advanced age who wanted to change theirs – as well as for all those who were happy with the status quo but liked change as a spectator sport. Kate, who supports me in all things, received this news in silence. Then she said:

'A whole *book?* But what would you say?'

Everyone was so different, she argued, that any attempt to lay down the law would be vulgar. I protested that it was a simple fact that on average people live longer than they thought they would last time they made any plans for the future. The actuaries at Aviva had recently told me I'd probably soldier on until I was 93 – and that knowledge should surely shape the decisions I made now.

Kate looked even crosser. One of the truths of life, she said, is that none of us knows when we will die. How could I write a book about having 33 years left, knowing that someone might be reading it who had just been diagnosed with terminal cancer?

I assured her I didn't want to upset anyone with cancer. My point was that many people, me included, arrived in their late 50s with no plans for the rest of their lives – and I wanted to write a book for them.

Here was an open goal. I was giving Kate the perfect opportunity to quote Woody Allen, which of course she did. 'The best way to make God laugh,' she said, 'is to tell Him your plans.'

I love my sister. I respect her. If Kate thinks something is a bad idea, then it probably is a bad idea. For the next few weeks I resolved not to write a book after all. The fact that I had changed my life was of no interest to anyone other than me. But then I thought: Fuck it. I had recently taught probability to a class of Year 9s. Probability, I explained to them, isn't certainty, but it is a way of assessing how likely a certain outcome is. I don't know when I will die. But there is a high probability I have a big slice of time left, which means it's not too late to make big changes to my life. Nothing is too late.

As I write that I realise it's rubbish. For me, it is too late to have more children. It's too late to train as a doctor, as that takes six years and I'd be almost 70 by the time I qualified. It's probably too late to become a professional athlete, but then given that I can't run, throw or catch that was probably never on the cards anyway.

It's not too late to move house, to have new relationships – or to start again in a new career. And if God wants to laugh at my plans, He can be my guest. The comedy of them isn't lost on me either.

In the autumn of 2016 I wrote a proselytising column in the *FT* announcing I was quitting the newspaper and explaining why: I was no longer getting better as a columnist; I longed to do something more useful; I wanted to start all over again at the bottom and learn something new. What I was trying to do was lure other people into quitting whatever they were up to and becoming teachers too.

In response, a columnist at the *Guardian* wrote a piece arguing that lots of middle-aged people fantasise about change but do nothing about it. The reason I'd managed to go through with it, Gaby Hinsliff concluded, was because I'd just got divorced. 'What's one more upheaval when your life is changing drastically anyway?' she wrote.

I read this with displeasure. Bloody columnists, I thought. Can't even get their facts right. I wasn't divorced – merely separated. And how dare she claim to understand my motivation better than I understood my own, especially given she'd never set eyes on me? My decision to become a teacher had absolutely nothing to do with my marital status. Why would it?

Looking back on it now, I have a nasty feeling she might have been partly right – it all was connected, though perhaps not in the way that she thought. The big changes in my life were ones I had no control over: my children grew up and my parents died, which meant by my late 50s I was less encumbered than I'd ever been. But if there was one self-inflicted change that tipped me over into ending my 32-year relationship with my employer, it was not separating from my husband, it was moving into a modern house.

Possibly I would be a teacher if I still lived in our old house in Highbury, though I doubt it. Its roots were deep. If I were still living there, I think I would still be stuck in a life that no longer suited me. But that's the odd thing about changing your life: it doesn't always begin quite where you expect it to.

1

Space

In August 2015 I left my husband for a 20-foot strip of bright orange Corian. It was an irregular thing to do but it was the best decision I'd taken since deciding to marry him 25 years earlier. The data suggests that women who do the more usual thing and leave their husbands for another man often regret it as the new model can turn out to be not that much of an improvement on the old one. I don't know the statistics for women who leave their husbands for coloured polymer counters as the data set must be small. But if my hunch is right, and I'm the only woman in the world ever to have done this, the stats tell me it can work out a lot better than you'd think.

Not only did spending all my life's savings on this orange strip and the modern house that encased it make me happier. It also helped my relationship with David – who is still technically my husband as neither of us can see the point in divorcing. More unexpectedly, the freedom that came from leaving the vertical Victorian houses I'd lived in all my life and moving to a horizontal modern space did something I can't quite understand, even now five years on. It released me from the force of habit that had defined my life until then.

Long ago, before there were any noticeable cracks in my marriage, I used to throw David's books away. Every evening he would come home from *Prospect*, the magazine he founded, with a bag full of review copies he'd been sent and add them to the waist-high piles that dotted the floor of his study.

On the second Sunday of every month a skip would arrive on our street for local residents to fill with their garden clippings and clapped-out Ikea furniture. I would wait for David to go off to his weekly game of football, load up a couple of bags and nip out to the skip. One day he came back unexpectedly and caught me on the front steps with four plastic carriers bulging with books. He was so intent on not missing the start of his game I don't think he noticed me, let alone wondered what I was doing. He never asked me about it. And because I did my pruning so deftly he never missed a single book. He didn't read much anyway; he was too busy.

Not only did he keep books, he kept articles from newspapers and magazines which he'd tear out and keep in tottering piles. He had so much stuff he eventually had to move his study into the largest room in our house to accommodate the paper – as well as the ancient cassette tapes, broken electronic kit, and trunks filled with his old reporter's notebooks. But mainly the problem was books, which I kept under control with trips to the skip – until one day the council canned the service, which forced me to make covert trips to the local rubbish dump instead, hiding David's books in the back of the car under garden trimmings and other legit things I was getting rid of.

If you had said that this act of subversion was an ominous sign – that what I was really trying to get rid of was my husband – I would have strongly denied it. Back then, throwing away was not about anything more profound than an incompatibility with clutter – or anything ugly. I have always had a fervid interest in my surroundings. I don't mind a bit of mess and am fine with dirt but I find it hard to relax if there is anything ugly nearby. As I sit writing this in the open-plan room in my Hackney house my eye alights on a bunch of purple, yellow and red tulips someone sent one of my daughters. In themselves they're well enough, but they don't go with the faded kilim rug. This pains me.

The obsession with interiors (and exteriors) started when I was a child. I spent the first 18 years of my life in an elegant if shabby Regency terraced house near Kentish Town that my Australian grandmother had bought in the 1950s for 500 quid. Almost before I'd learnt to read, Mum had taught me the superiority of square-paned windows and of egg-and-dart cornices. She was a property fiend, an early adopter of property pornography, and through her I discovered the bottomless pleasure of the smudgy, stamp-sized photos of houses for sale in the local newspapers. This has become a lifelong enslavement – and as the quality of the porn has improved, with the black-and-white photos giving way to colour and then to online slide shows and videos, my dependency has grown.

Back then we'd sometimes go and look at places Mum had found, 'just for fun'. And what fun it was to imagine ourselves living in the water mill in Suffolk that she once took us to, which we had neither the money nor any intention to buy.

In the early 1980s, at the age of 23 and on a banker's salary, I started the property hunt for real. Every evening after work Mum and I visited flats in Camden Town, finally settling on a dingy one-bedroom garden flat in Albert Street which I bought for £27,000. Dad and I set to with cans of white emulsion, undercoat and gloss, and there began an enduring relationship with DIY. Dad taught me how to paint quickly and just about well enough so the result didn't look truly awful, a technique that has served me well over the years, as it has meant no decorating job is too daunting to start – or to finish. If a job's worth doing, it's worth doing badly, he would say.

Having bought the flat in the depths of a recession I sold it seven years later to move to Brussels, where I was to report on the new European Union. The property market was by then booming, and along came the comedian Julian Clary, who bought it for almost four times what I'd paid for it. I was barely 30 but had made as much money in one lucky transaction as in six years working as a journalist. I had won the property lottery and was set up for life.

A couple of years ago I drove down Albert Street with Maud, my second daughter. As we passed number 5 I pointed out the place I'd lived in my 20s, bought when I was slightly younger than she then was.

Maud looked at it in amazement.

'What? How did you afford it?'

I told her it was different then. Property was cheap.

Buying a flat in a pretty street in Camden in 1983 cost four times my salary. Buying the same flat now would cost twenty times hers. We contemplate this glumly.

'Bloody hell,' she says.

'Bloody hell,' I agree.

When I returned from Brussels two years later, by then married and with six-month-old Rose, David and I bought our first family house in a quiet street in Islington. It was a bit down on its luck as the old man who had lived there had died and the house was a mess. But the rooms were big, there was a conservatory and a garden. We got it fixed up and I was happy there.

Happy, that is, until the house on the other side of the street came on the market three years later. It was a beauty, semi-detached with arched windows and a long, wild garden that backed onto the churchyard beyond. On the downside, it had an outside loo, no heating and a hole in the roof through which you could see the sky. At that point I had three children under the age of four and David had just left his job and was working 18 hours a day to get his new magazine off the ground. It wasn't an obviously sensible move, but I wanted the house and I persuaded him we ought to buy it. David, who likes change in general and had a very robust attitude to risk but no interest whatsoever in exteriors or interiors, agreed on the condition he didn't need to think about it or do anything about it himself. We got a bridging loan and bought it.

Every day before work I crossed the road to visit the building site, usually carrying at least one child, to tell the electrician where to put the sockets and the plumber which way round to install the bath. Every day after work I gleefully inspected progress. I threw myself into taming the garden, letting the children watch *Postman Pat* on an endless loop while I hacked at branches, mowed and planted.

It was an enchanting place to live. For my 40th birthday David commissioned a family photograph taken in the garden. Six of us squeezed onto a small bench, all smiling broadly and apparently naturally – apart from Stan who had one fat finger stuck in his mouth, too young to know the drill.

In 2000, six months after the photo was taken, the property itch got to me again. Looking back now, all this constant moving seems suspect. Was I so restless because I realised something wasn't quite right with my life and my marriage and by moving house I thought I'd make us different and somehow better? Possibly; though I fear the truth was far shallower than that: I just loved property.

Now with four children, I had a more-or-less legitimate reason for another move as we needed more bedrooms. After an immersion in the top property porn of the time – freebie property magazines that were shoved through the letter box – I spotted a house both bigger and cheaper up the road. It had wide steps up to the door, many rooms with doors that closed and a separate flat downstairs that our nanny and her boyfriend could live in. This, I decided, was going to be our permanent home. We now had a big family and this place was going to be its proper headquarters.

For once, David expressed an opinion: he liked the new place because it was solid and didn't shake when he went upstairs. I liked its solidity too – and was prepared to swap the romance of the old house for the idea that this new one was big enough to keep us safe.

Subsequently I discovered that size of house cuts both ways. It may have kept us safe from the world outside, but it also kept us safe from each other. As the children grew older and became teenagers an average evening at number 52 would not find the family amiably playing Scrabble or even gathering passively around the TV to watch *Friends*. After a quick supper cooked by me – soggy leek-and-bacon pasta or chicken nuggets and broccoli – we dispersed. David retreated to his study at the very top of the house, the girls to their separate rooms to do conscientious homework and talk to friends on MSN Messenger, and the boys to play *Call of Duty* on the consoles I thought I'd hidden. I stayed in the kitchen, often tired and resentful, on my own call of duty clearing up the kitchen. Sometimes I did this alone, but increasingly Dad sat at the table too.

7

When Mum died suddenly and entirely unexpectedly in 2006, I vowed to myself that I would look after my devastated father. He lived about a mile away and in the early days, when his legs were still up to it, he'd put on his ancient brown overcoat, take his walking stick and climb the hill to have supper with us. I had extended this open invitation as evidence of the strong family I wanted us to be, with me at the centre dispensing food and love to older and younger generations simultaneously. The reality was different – I would snap at everyone while Dad sat morosely at the table, head down and contemplating his jumper. He was a gentle person who hated sharp words and his mood lowered with every testy exchange between me and David or me and the children. I was cross with the children for not being nicer, cross with David for never helping and being so often absent, cross with myself for being the least nice of the lot, and cross with Dad for being a gloomy witness to the everyday squabbles of family life.

During our 15 years in the big, solid family house, David and I started to fall apart. I don't know why a marriage ever ends (even less do I know how one ever stays together), but the two of us, through years of over-work, distraction and mutual neglect, had somehow lost the thread that had once tied us to each other so securely. The house was oblivious to our distress and doggedly continued in its role as family headquarters. It was big enough to accommodate any dysfunction we threw at it; after our nanny moved out David moved into the basement flat, sometimes coming up for family suppers to join his grumpy wife, his grumpy teenage children and his frail father-in-law, who was not only depressed but was becoming increasingly confused.

I don't know what Dad thought about David moving downstairs or the evident unravelling of my marriage. He didn't say, and I was grateful for our safe conversations about his shopping lists or whatever novel he'd been reading. This sort of denial has a lot to be said for it. It was an unspoken, sympathetic agreement that prodding at my unhappiness was not going to make it go away.

This arrangement, with me upstairs and David downstairs, was so irregular the children sometimes found its ambiguity hard to explain to their friends, but it just about worked. With David in the basement the resentment that had been a growing feature of my marriage receded a little. It gave us both space from the other while at the same time allowed us to act as if we were still more or less a normal family.

Left to his own devices in the basement David's piles of paper got higher. What was happening upstairs was, I now see, a sign that I was tipping over the edge.

The madness of my throwing-away binges was disguised by the fact that then, in 2013, I was bang on trend. I had been throwing things away in a small way all my life, but the arrival on the scene of Marie Kondo, the dogmatic Japanese minimalist, was just what I had been waiting for. Kondo and her crazy book gave me permission to go much deeper than I'd ever dared before. I was so excited by *The Life-Changing Magic of Tidying* I bought ten copies and gave them to all my friends and relations for Christmas. My sister, Kate, who lived in a cluttered but beautiful house with her poet husband (who had a garage piled to the roof with rusted lawnmowers and broken chairs), looked at the book distrustfully. 'There's something decadent,' she said, 'about all that hysterical throwing away.'

Marie Kondo's bar was a high one. She instructed me to get rid of anything that did not give me joy. At that time, with my marriage on the ropes, still in the same old job I'd been in for decades, looking after a frail and fading father and with children peeling away to go to university, very little gave me joy. So I threw almost the whole house out. I went through every room and every cupboard. Every weekend I drove another carful of my dwindling belongings to the dump. At the same time my DIY urges, always quite strong, were getting out of control. I repainted the whole house and taught myself to wallpaper and upholster. There was no calm anywhere. Everywhere were boxes of upholstery tacks and half-empty cans of paint.

Anyone looking on should have been able to see that there was something wrong. It did not occur to me then that the problem wasn't too many belongings. There were other changes I needed to make, but felt I couldn't, mustn't – and didn't even want to think about. My marriage to David was not only an institution, it was my whole adult life. The house we lived in was the receptacle for all this and I was determined we would go on living there for at least another five years until all the children were through university and settled. It was my job and my duty as their mother and as joint head of the institution to keep everything as much the same as it always had been. I believed this so fundamentally, I never discussed it with anyone (apart from with David, just once, who acquiesced to the idea of soldiering on for a few more years), because there was nothing to say. Job, marriage, big house: the framework of our lives must stay just the same.

And then one day, out of the blue, Maud introduced me to the crack cocaine of property pornography: the Modern House. I inhaled the website with its minimalist houses made of polished concrete and glass with their Danish mid-century furniture and dangling houseplants. I could have spent the rest of the day entranced and gawping had it not been for Maud's insistence that I focus on a particular house she'd found.

'You'll love this,' she said.

From the outside the Framehouse was a wooden triangle, a fancy garden shed. Inside there was a big open space with glass walls onto the garden and a long strip of orange Corian running down the middle.

'Let's go and see it,' I said. 'Just for fun.'

One sunny spring day just after Easter in 2015 Maud and I got in the car and drove three miles east to a narrow, grubby lane, at the bottom of which, past a car body shop, was what appeared to be a stained, oversized wooden shed in the shape of a triangle. We stepped over the threshold and there, right in front of us, was the stretch of bright orange worktop under a double-height sloping glass roof leading to a pond outside where orange goldfish swam.

Any lingering fun stopped at once. It was replaced by an earth-moving *coup de foudre* that I have never experienced before or since – either with bricks and mortar or with flesh and blood. I knew for sure: I absolutely had to live in this house. It was tattier than in the pictures. Outside the wood in the garden was rotten, and a broken drainpipe discharged water through a rusty old basketball hoop. I didn't care. I felt a yearning so powerful I must have had an inkling that buying this house would change more than my address.

We went home in silence with me glumly contemplating the impossibility of buying the Framehouse. There was no way I could evict David and the children from their home. Back in the Highbury kitchen I showed Stan, who was loafing around avoiding doing any work for his AS levels, the place Maud and I had seen, just for fun. He was used to 'fun' of this sort and seemed bored by it – until he looked at the picture I was thrusting under his nose.

Stan: I've been there.
Me: What? When?
Stan: I went to a party there in Year 6.
Me: Really? What did you think of it?
Stan: It's the coolest house ever.

Me (*with trepidation*): What would you think if we sold this house and lived there?

Stan: Yeah, cool.

Emboldened by the unexpected turn this conversation had taken, I went downstairs to put the idea to David. For years we had avoided any discussion about our future together. We'd implicitly agreed that we would stay in the uneasy state of together-but-apart at least until all the children had gone to university – but hadn't talked about what we'd do then. But now here I was jumping the gun by at least three years, saying I wanted to move east at once. There was no need to say the rest of it, because we both knew it too well. Our marriage was irredeemably broken and I had had enough of pretending.

David looked up from his laptop screen, seemed briefly surprised and then said: Yes, fine. I should have predicted that it would have been this easy. One of the nicest things about him is that he nearly always says yes, no matter how hare-brained the question. I said we could split the money from the house in half and he could buy somewhere nice of his own. I pointed out that he might rather like living somewhere where his belongings would be beyond the reach of the woman who was always trying to throw them out.

Even Dad, who had taught me all my life that the only important thing was to hold your marriage together for the sake of your children, gave his permission. When I showed him photos of the place, he said Mum (who had by then been dead for nearly ten years) would have loved the house and been right behind me – which was the nicest thing he could possibly have said.

The story seemed to be this. I was going to leave my husband and the edifice of our family life, not for another man, but for a wooden house. Our existing home, which I'd clung to as a life raft for everyone, turned out to be something that all six of us were prepared to leave and to swim off somewhere else. It was as easy as that.

Only it didn't turn out to be quite so easy. I wasn't the only person to fall for the Framehouse; my low offer was rejected and half a dozen suitors were invited to submit sealed bids. I did my sums, putting in my half-share of the family home and adding all my savings. It was an astoundingly large amount of money for a glorified garden shed down a rubbish-strewn lane, but I submitted it anyway.

On the day of the sealed bids, I was nominally at work, but incapable of doing any as I needed to check my phone several times a minute. At last, towards teatime the message from the estate agents came.

Hi Lucy. I have good news for you. Can you call me?

I remember having to go to the loo to hide how much I was shaking. I didn't feel any of the jubilation that I'd expected to feel – I felt only panic. I had somehow, inadvertently and by dint of a text from an estate agent, just taken the biggest decision of my life. Deciding to get married 25 years earlier had not seemed terribly momentous as I was already pregnant. Deciding to join the *FT* was also a no-brainer – the more I thought of it, I had spent my entire life without taking any difficult decisions at all.

Now here I was having bet everything on a house that was inconveniently placed, further from work and off the Tube network; that was overpriced, that torched my savings, and that, most importantly, made my separation from David official and probably permanent. All for what? For a worktop?

The surveyor gave me a perfect opportunity to back out. I've just looked for the report I conscientiously commissioned but seem to have thrown it away. No matter – I remember its damning detail well enough with its page after page of close-up pictures of bad wiring and dodgy sections of wood. At the time I read the report in dismay and rang its author to remonstrate.

Me: Is your report so negative because that's your job, or do you genuinely think the house is a dud?
Surveyor (*very slowly*): Do. Not. Buy. This. House.

I showed the report to Marcus Lee, the architect who'd built it, lived in it and was now selling it. Would he consider lowering the price? No, he wouldn't.

I could have walked away, but I didn't. Damn the surveyor, I thought, I was going to buy it anyway. She didn't understand beauty; I did.

Meanwhile, David had found a nice flat in Hampstead and seemed upbeat. But my anxiety was growing with every box I packed in Highbury. For a start, I was moving further away from Dad, who by then was 89 and needed driving everywhere. Ferrying him to and fro from Hackney was going to involve an hour and a half driving a day. If anything bad happened it would take me longer to get to him. This was not the right time to be extricating myself from my house and, as if to prove the point, two weeks before we moved Dad got pneumonia and could not be left alone. I installed him on our sofa, wrapped him in blankets and went on miserably filling the packing cases, dividing my adult life in half while my father slept fitfully on the sofa.

On a hot day in the middle of August, two pantechnicons parked outside the house. David's stuff went into one, mine into the other. Arty and Maud took me out to breakfast and then Maud helped all day, vacuuming and dusting as furniture was carried out. I was aware of our roles shifting as if I was the child and she the parent, practical and intent on keeping me calm. When the last belongings had been carted down the steps I went back into the house one final time.

What hit me didn't feel like grief: it was something more elemental. I leant against the wall in the empty sitting room and howled. I had done something irreversible. This was my family, my life, my marriage and I had carelessly and selfishly thrown it all away.

Sometimes I marvel at my own fickleness. In the 15-minute drive from one London borough to another I pulled myself together. By the time we had turned into the narrow lane and my belongings started arriving at the Framehouse, my spirits were soaring. I was like a child and this was the most exciting Christmas of my life. Against every probability, I had escaped.

A few days later I went with some of the children to visit David in his flat and see how he was doing. An entire room was filled with cardboard boxes full of books, which I was convinced (correctly, as it happens) would remain unpacked for many years. For the first time in my life these were not my concern. It occurred to me both that I had never made any noticeable inroads into David's stuff and that I hadn't thrown David himself away either. There he was, looking proudly proprietorial in his own flat. This was a new beginning for everyone.

For me the problem with this new beginning was that it turned out to be damper and even more expensive than I'd bargained for. It rained that first week and water ran down my bedroom wall. There was a leak in the water pipe outside, and the architect couldn't remember where the stopcock was. Everything the surveyor thought was wrong turned out to be wrong. The wood cladding did not keep the water out. The cracked lead flat roofs at the sides didn't keep it out either, sending water running down behind the kitchen units and fusing the electricity. The air source heat pump had a mind of its own, so sometimes the heating worked and sometimes it didn't. The house wasn't on the gas mains, and in the middle of cooking the Calor cylinders gave out, meaning I had to drive to the petrol station to get a replacement, which was too heavy for me to lift into the car and I had to beg a perfect stranger to help me.

Usually love at first sight fizzles out but occasionally it turns into something lasting and deep. And this is how it has been between me and the Framehouse. Our relationship is unconditional, in sickness and in health. This is just as well, as the house has turned out to be a lot sicker than I'd thought and sometimes seems to have borderline personality disorder – but that doesn't change my feelings.

The Framehouse gives me pleasure every time I enter it. Every time I go downstairs for a cup of tea, I am lifted by the orange. Every time I lie in the bath and look through sloping glass at trees outside I think how lucky I am to live there. The way the light slants through the glass roof. The way the kitchen and the garden are one space.

I now laugh at my old fear that I was somehow throwing my family away: most of my children are very much around, in the way that twentysomethings tend to be, but the house has created a different relationship between me and them. They did not grow up here; they have adult bedrooms, which they occupy when it suits them. They like the house and are amused and only slightly exasperated by my irrational passion for it. In the early days I would drag random people off the street and give them a tour while my children would roll their eyes.

David comes round for supper sometimes, lugging a bag of newspaper cuttings to read in case the conversation lags. But then he goes home, leaving me free to arrange my belongings (which are now mounting up again) as it suits me.

Part of the liberation that happened that day in August was caused simply by leaving the old house. I had cut loose both from an edifice and from the institution of marriage – and felt instantly lighter for it. Wherever I'd moved to I would have felt freer, but the quality of the lightness was also due to the peculiar nature of the space itself.

With every other house I've lived in I have got to work at once trying to impose my personality on it. This is partly because all these houses were much the same – and the same as houses in thousands of streets all over London. I now see my attempts to make mine individual, mainly through subtly different shades of Farrow & Ball paint, were comically conformist, and even the William Morris wallpaper I glued to the walls or the banana-yellow lino on the kitchen floor weren't as radical as all that. Either way, we were living in a regular middle-class family house and had little choice but to live in it more or less like a regular middle-class London family.

With my new house there was no question of my imposing myself on it. Its personality was so strong I hoped any imposition would run the other way. The house was inarguably cool and I thought I might become a bit cooler by dint of living there. Alas, the image of me reflected back in the big mirrored doors in the hallway in the early days looked disappointingly familiar, and even now, several years later, there are still no signs of advancing coolness, though plenty of advancing age.

While the Framehouse has not changed how I look, it has changed how I live. There are fewer walls that constrain me and more light. I move from one thing to another – from cooking to working to eating to talking to gardening. I am more likely to invite people round for supper (and am still keen to show the house off six years in) but also find the house's company so stimulating I often prefer pottering alone. I wake in the morning in the modern bedroom on my own and still feel a sense of possibility and promise. The Framehouse is surprising and quixotic and doesn't abide by normal rules. It is as if it issues a daily invitation to me to follow suit.

Would I have changed the rest of my life if I still lived in Highbury? This is a stupid question, in that there is no knowing for sure. But my guess is that in that unchanged house, with its solidity and safety, I might well have gone on living a largely unchanged life. The Framehouse is not solid and, as it's made entirely from wood and has dodgy wiring, not remotely safe either. But in moving here I proved to myself that change is possible, that it comes at a price, but that it can be very good indeed.

2

Fearless

In early May 2016, after more than two weeks in the Whitting-
ton Hospital with defunct kidneys, heart failure, pneumonia
and a twice-broken hip, Dad gave up the ghost.

Kate, my brother Roland, my cousin Liz, and I had been
taking it in turns to sit by his bed day and night in a room in
which the only ornament – a black TV screen high on the wall
facing his bed – was clad in a white paper shroud. This was
because one evening Dad, who had eaten nothing for days
and whose grip on the world was loosening, was sent into a fit
of King Lear-like madness by the terror of the black rectangle. I climbed up on his bed, took a roll of surgical tape and
paper towels and made the telly a makeshift cover. Freed from
his terrors, Dad reached for my hand and went to sleep.

On the 18th morning I arrived at 7am to take over from
Kate who had been doing the night shift. She was standing in
the corridor outside his room with her back to me talking to a
nurse. I didn't need to see my sister's face to know our beloved
father was dead. I had missed him by just five minutes.

Through her sobs Kate told me his death was beautiful. Dad was like a boat that had slipped its moorings and drifted out to sea.

Three days later I went back to work. I did this because it was what Dad himself would have done. He didn't like a fuss, and thought it was important to get on with life and do whatever one was supposed to be doing. I also did it because I'd long since understood that one of the functions of work is to serve as a distraction when life goes wrong. I could either sit at home poleaxed with grief or I could divert myself by going through the motions of work. The latter seemed the better option.

Only it turned out not to be. I got into the office and sat at my desk next to a young political reporter who was talking excitedly about having just spotted a George Galloway campaign bus near Ladbroke Grove trying to rustle up support for the mayoral elections.

So what? I wanted to shout.

All around me my colleagues were looking busy and important. I scrolled through the news in search of something to write about and a thought presented itself to me.

I can't do this anymore.

As I entertained the idea, it grew to fill my whole head. I had to get out. But what could I do? I was 57 years old and had spent my whole life doing one thing. And at that precise moment this one thing was something I was not only fed up with but felt was doing me actual harm.

When Dad was a couple of years younger than I was then, he'd also run into a brick wall at work. He'd taken early retirement from the job he'd done all his life as librarian and secretary of the Institute of Historical Research at the University of London. He'd been complaining of a fizziness in his head which made him unable to concentrate on the meticulous indexing of historical documents which had been his life's work. He had a couple of brain scans which found nothing, but the fizziness had continued and so he quit. It now seems to me he was probably depressed, but that wasn't the sort of thing a no-nonsense Australian male was going to have any truck with in the 1970s.

With me it was different. I don't think I was especially depressed and there was no fizzing in my head; I was just unhappy and monumentally stuck. I had been doing the same thing for too long and was worn out mentally, physically and emotionally.

I don't know how hard Dad found it to leave his job as he never discussed it. He dealt with the next 35 years by getting on a bus or train every morning and going to an art gallery where he would stand for hours, carefully taking stock of each picture. He was a scholar and a collector; in my bottom drawer at home is a shoe box of his containing several hundred postcards of self-portraits which he'd carefully arranged alphabetically and, when there was more than one portrait by the same artist, chronologically. I've just taken the box out of its drawer and felt a prick of guilt that under my careless stewardship the contents have got jumbled. Under the tab that says REMBRANDT in Dad's shaky writing, the handsome figure of Max Ernst seems to have taken up residence.

Dad didn't say if this arduous cultural retirement suited him as it was obvious it did. It was equally obvious that something similar would be a disaster for me. I had an *FT* pension and could in theory have done the same thing, but my appetite for galleries is limited, having been put off them by overexposure as a child. In any case, there was no way I was going to retire. I enjoy pottering at home reading and gardening and decorating as much as the next person – or, judging by effort expended, considerably more than the next person. But I don't want to devote my life to these things – I like doing them in addition to work, in between the gaps of work, and, most particularly, as a reward for completed work. Without work, leisure makes no sense.

David once said to me, as he observed me doing some late-night DIY while he sat up in bed reading a newspaper, that all this frenetic activity was because I couldn't stand the emptiness of my own thoughts. I wasn't particularly offended by this, because I don't think there is anything shameful about constant activity. The rest of the world may have converted to mindfulness and to seeing some sort of virtue in doing things slowly, but I am holding firm. Doing lots of things – and doing them fast so that you can do more of them – has always struck me as a whole lot better than slouching around taking your time or, worse, not doing things at all.

Dad's death made my natural propensity for action even stronger. It also made me think that starting all over again at the bottom in a new career was not only possible but was the only sensible thing to do. Death is meant to make you think that you must seize the day, as life is fleeting and any of us could die at any minute – but watching Dad dwindling had the opposite effect on me. If Dad, at the age of 90, could go on living for a full two weeks with most of his vital organs on the blink and with no sustenance save the odd sip of water from a baby's cup or a teaspoon, then that made me feel practically immortal. But what on earth was I going to do with all the time I had left?

Looking back, it was always on the cards that I'd end up a teacher. My mother was one and my oldest daughter Rose is one and these things tend to run in families. Mum taught English at Camden School for Girls, the famously liberal grammar that I went to in the 1970s. This arrangement should have been hideous for both of us, especially as I was a naughty adolescent, doing badly academically and often to be found smoking Player's No. 6 outside the back gate.

Mum never told me what this was like for her, but from my side it was great. Being Mrs Kellaway's daughter made me special. Mum taught with a blast of enthusiasm and was adored by all her students. If the tools of motivation are sticks and carrots, her approach was to provide pupils with an all-you-can-eat buffet of carrots and forget sticks entirely. This way she managed to get the naughtiest girls, whose hair was blue, who smoked dope on the way to school and who had renounced homework altogether, to write long essays on *Paradise Lost*. No matter how chaotic these pieces of work were, Mum would always find something to admire, writing 'Lovely!' in the margin and detailed encouragement at the bottom of each student's work. Whenever I meet Camden girls now, nearly half a century later, they are never especially interested in what I've been up to, they just want to reminisce about Mrs Kellaway. It's gratifying, if ever so slightly tiresome.

I admired my mum, but I never wanted to be like her. I looked at the piles of books she sat marking until midnight. I watched her run herself ragged putting on a school production of 'The Hollow Men', getting so frazzled that at home she would bang saucepan lids and snap at us. I thought there was something disproportionate about the effort she put into teaching, that she was throwing away her talents on these girls – it was pearls before swine.

I also could not believe how little she earned. I wanted my working life to be as unlike Mum's as possible. When I left university, I got a job at J.P. Morgan. My starting salary, as a know-nothing 21-year-old, was slightly more than what Mum got as surely one of the best teachers in the borough.

Banking turned out to be grim – a lethal combination of stress and boredom. I disliked it so much I sometimes went to the loo not to wee but to weep. I knew I had to get out before the money became a habit but had no idea what else to do.

Journalism did not seem like a great fit as I'd never been drawn to it at university, was slow at reading and writing, and wasn't noticeably interested in the news. But a few of my friends had become journalists and they appeared to be having a jollier time at work than anyone else I knew.

By the age of 25 I had wangled a job at the *Financial Times* after a brief stint on the *Investors Chronicle* – and there I stayed for the next 32 years.

What kept me going all that time? What is anyone's motivation for being a hack? I've just asked David – who is still, 40 years on, writing about social trends – why he became a journalist all those years ago and why he's still at it.

He said what I knew he was going to say: he wanted to change the world. He wanted to be in the thick of things: he covered Chernobyl, Hillsborough, the miners' strike, the Berlin Wall – jobs don't get more exciting than that.

My motivation was quite different. I was frightened of news, and of missing the story. It never occurred to me for a single second I might be capable of changing the world; I wasn't even quite sure which bits were in need of changing. My interests have always been, in the language of economics, micro. I was curious about people. I liked interviewing them and noticing little things about them. I discovered I had a knack for making fun of things – and of my luckless interviewees – and liked trying to make readers laugh.

What sustained me all those years was a personality flaw that is common in journalists. I was both insecure and a show-off. I wanted the limelight, but also suffered from imposter syndrome. The great motivation for me, and the reason I worked so hard, was fear of being found out. I could hardly believe I was on such a revered newspaper and was getting away with it. I dreaded making mistakes (which I did too often) but, more than that, I dreaded being no good.

From the very first article I wrote I thought: Why does anyone take me seriously writing this, when I don't have a clue? Why would someone want to read a piffling column by me about the conversations in office loos, when it's neither funny nor clever?

This fear of being rubbish, though painful, was single-handedly responsible for my not being rubbish. When I was done writing a column, I didn't press send but spent another couple of hours – or however long I had until deadline – going over every word, expending a prodigious amount of effort in an attempt to make it look effortless.

I have asked around and it seems this is quite common among journalists – especially female ones. If I didn't know better, I'd think it was outrageous that women end up feeling like insecure imposters while male colleagues glide around complacently, puffed up on ill-placed confidence. But experience tells me that insecurity can be a secret weapon. Anything that makes you get better must be good – so long as the psychic damage that it results in is manageable.

And mostly for me it was manageable. I generally wasn't lying awake at night (or rather, I was, but that was usually because

I was either worrying about my children or about not being able to sleep and being tired the next day). Instead, insecurity allowed me to view my own work with mild disdain and be hyper-sensitive to its flaws. This had the advantage that I managed to fix many of them before anyone else got to see them.

The other thing that kept me writing was equally unattractive: I was profoundly impressed by the sight of my own name in a newspaper. I enjoyed the way strangers' faces would rearrange themselves when I announced I worked for the *FT*. Quite often people, particularly men, would look surprised, in which case I took pleasure in biting their heads off.

Patronising man at dinner party: Do you work outside the home?

Me: Yes, I'm a journalist.

Man: Ah. What do you write about?

Me: I'm a columnist on the *FT*.

Man: Ah! (*pause*) Are you freelance?

Me: No. I've been on staff for many years.

Man: Oh, really? What did you say your name was?

Me: Lucy Kellaway.

Man (*expression changes from boredom to mild deference*): I think I may have read you.

Me: I'm curious: why did you ask if I was freelance?

Man (*pauses*): Well, lots of people are.

Me: Actually, on the *FT* almost no one is, so I wonder what it is about me that made you wonder?

Man (*prevaricating*): Well, perhaps you don't look like my idea of a typical *FT* journalist.

Me: What does a typical *FT* journalist look like?

Man (*squirming*): I don't know.

Me: Male?

Man: No! Not at all. Look, I don't know how we got on to this …

Status really mattered to me. I wouldn't have admitted it at the time, but I wanted to be seen to be successful. I thought that I wouldn't get invited to things and people wouldn't be interested in talking to me if I didn't have the badge of an *FT* columnist. I remember going to a party in the mid-1990s given by some grand contact of David's and being approached by an American economist who worked at the International Monetary Fund who told me how much he and his colleagues had enjoyed an interview I'd done with the disgraced head of the European Bank for Reconstruction and Development, Jacques Attali. The fact that I can remember this compliment and how exalted it made me feel a quarter of a century later strikes me as both pathetic and shameful. But that was how it was.

Fear and status weren't the only things that kept me at it. I also enjoyed the writing itself. I was slow at assembling words but liked polishing them and, on a good day, became so immersed I experienced that intense thing that someone has helpfully found a name for: flow.

The work was agreeable – and so was the way I frittered time in the office when not working. I was surrounded by clever, funny people, and I spent large parts of every day sitting in the canteen with them drinking Diet Coke and chatting. How could I not enjoy that?

Twenty years into this accidental career, things were going better than I had ever thought they would. I had interviewed all sorts of interesting people. The column I'd been writing for a decade had become a fixture in the paper. I had invented a fictional character, a ghastly jargon-spouting manager, and the columns I wrote on his behalf had become a minor cult hit. I still felt like an interloper, but in a manageable sort of way.

Then one morning in January 2006, Mum woke up early, went upstairs in her nightdress to make herself a cup of tea, had an aneurism, and died.

As I tried to march on through the torrent of shock and grief that followed, I decided I didn't want to be a journalist anymore. If my brilliant, vibrant mother was no longer there, I needed to try, if not to become her, then to continue the work she had started. An unexpected and unwanted thought presented itself to me: perhaps I should be a teacher.

The feeling didn't last. I talked to friends about it, none of whom thought it a good idea. I looked up some PGCE courses but quickly lost heart. I was then 47, which I decided was too old to do something so radical.

What I didn't know then was that I wasn't too old to stop being a journalist and start again as a teacher – I was too young. My youngest child was only eight, my job still suited me and I still needed the money. More important, I still wanted the status that the job gave me. I wanted to be someone. Back then it hadn't occurred to me that a teacher, with the notable exception of Mum herself, was anyone at all. For the next decade, I forgot about teaching. I went on, mainly happily, doing what I had always done.

I gave no further thought to teaching until June 2013 when Rose left university and joined Teach First, set up to encourage bright graduates to spend two years as teachers in challenging schools. She was placed in a comprehensive in Leeds that was so tough that the word 'challenging' didn't begin to cover it. Every night I would ring her, eager for stories of the fights that broke out in the classroom and wanting to understand how on earth she was going about interesting her unruly charges in the reign of Edward I.

Through her I became fixated on the importance of education and outraged at how little of it so many children in the UK get. She told me that no one in her school had ever got an A* in history GCSE – which made no sense, given the size of the school. Some of the children, she said, came to school hungry and had multiple social problems. Some were out of control, leaving the teachers so busy putting out fires that getting any actual teaching done was virtually impossible.

The job of teaching these children mattered so much – why was it so hard to get anyone to do it? If someone set up

Teach Last, I said, I'd be its first recruit. I didn't mean this as a joke, but Rose laughed anyway.

At Christmas in her first year as a teacher one particularly difficult boy gave her a card on which he'd written: 'You're awesome, Miss.' I don't think it's the done thing to feel jealous of your own children, but as I looked at his backward-sloping script something that felt like envy presented itself to me, alongside a large helping of pride. It seemed to me that Rose had done more good in the first term of her working life than I'd done in 30 years of mine. When I said as much to her she got annoyed, and she still gets cross if she hears me running down journalism. I don't mean to run it down – it was just that what she was doing seemed to me to be so indisputably, undeniably useful, whereas I was sitting around wondering whether I could get away with writing yet another column on office Christmas parties.

A couple of years before this, sometime after my 50th birthday, my job had started to pall on me. The two things that held me to it – fear and status – were both losing their grip, and without them it wasn't clear what the point of it all was.

The loss of fear had snuck up on me unawares. One evening I was sitting next to a man at dinner who was telling me that the law firm where he worked routinely got rid of people in their 50s as they'd become too expensive and too lazy – they were no longer afraid of anything so they didn't work hard enough.

At first I felt mild outrage, but then it occurred to me that this was precisely what had happened to me. Somewhere along the way I'd stopped worrying about getting found out – if I had got away with it for 30 years, it was looking increasingly unlikely that someone was going to blow the whistle now. I no longer felt sick every time I'd finished writing something, neither did I wait in dread until an editor read it to say that it was OK. Instead I would file a column and shrug, usually thinking: Not great, but it'll probably do.

You might have thought being released from fear would be a good thing – but it wasn't. Fear for me was the flip side of caring, and so if I was no longer afraid it meant I didn't really care much anymore. And if I didn't care what was the point of all these words, all these opinions for the sake of opinions?

This lack of fear was starting to get me in trouble. A year or two before I quit journalism I was asked to give a talk to benefactors at Lady Margaret Hall, my old Oxford college. Public speaking used to fill me with such terror I would wildly over-rehearse, lie awake the night before and then have to fortify myself with beta blockers before standing up to speak.

About 20 years ago, I remember cycling off to give a speech to bankers, and as I rounded St Paul's, rehearsing the speech in my head one last time, I was nearly knocked off my bike by a cement mixer. Once I'd collected myself from the shock of almost being flattened I thought how stupid it was to have no fear of cycling in London – which is fantastically dangerous and might lead to death – yet be petrified of talking in front of a couple of dozen adults – which is entirely safe and the very worst thing that could happen is that a few people are slightly bored. I knew rationally this was the case. In practice it made no difference.

Two decades on, the night before my Oxford speech I slept perfectly soundly. On the train I put the finishing touches to a hasty speech that I thought was comically self-deprecating, comparing the frumpiness of the college in my day to its current much improved, less exclusive, state.

I felt no fear at all as I stood up in the wood-panelled dining hall surrounded by portraits of former principals, staring down balefully at the black-tie diners. The careless anecdotes that had seemed funny to me on the train turned out to be less so to this audience, who were mainly my contemporaries and who took me to be variously saying they were frumpy, dim and insular. As I finished, two red-faced men from the audience stormed high table, shouting in my face and showering me in furious spittle. This was quite an achievement as the point of the speech was to encourage guests to dig deep; what I'd actually achieved was to offend the largest benefactors so mortally that the fundraising committee called an emergency midnight session to see what could be done to repair the damage.

On the train on my way back to London the next day, having passed a sleepless night in the principal's lodgings, I reflected on what had gone wrong. If only I had been a little more fearful, I would have planned more carefully, taken fewer risks, and the evening would have gone off a whole lot better.

*

At the same time as losing my fear, something else was unravelling: my preoccupation with status. I was no longer impressed that I worked at the *FT* and didn't expect anyone else to be. The glamour that had once held me in its thrall had worn away to nothing. The doors my job opened to me were ones I no longer wanted to pass through. The penny had taken almost two decades to drop, but I'd worked out that those parties that I needed an *FT* badge to get invited to were ones that I had never enjoyed going to. I was no longer cheered if anyone said they'd liked what I'd written – if I didn't rate the work myself, it didn't matter to me if anyone else did.

Increasingly, I was feeling queasy about how I spent my time. There were whole days frittered away on enervating sessions of Twitter and aimless gossiping with colleagues. As I cycled home after a bad bout of idleness I often thought: I really need to find something different to do.

Despite this I kept going. The freedom suited me, as it always had. Being a columnist in charge of your own time was a gift when the children were young and went on being a gift when my father was old. My colleagues got used to hearing one-sided calls that sounded like this:

Me: Hello, Dad. Where are you?
(*pause*)
Me: Which bus are you on?
(*pause*)

Me: Ah. Can you remember how long you've been on it?

(*pause*)

Me: Don't worry, Dad. Can you ask the driver where you are and ring me back?

(*pause*)

Me: No, your home is Canonbury Square.

Sometimes I'd leave work in the middle of the day to go and help him. Sometimes I didn't turn up at all and wrote my columns from Dad's flat.

And then Dad died.

His death exacerbated everything that I'd been feeling already. It also changed the practicalities of my life. For the first time since Rose had been born a quarter of a century earlier I was no longer a carer. All my working time was mine, to do whatever I liked with it.

In the week after his death I found myself looking up PGCE courses, and once again I saw the young faces of trainees on the recruitment ads, and again thought I'd left it too late. But then I thought of Rose and the shortage of teachers and rang the government's helpline.

Me: I'm 57 and am thinking of becoming a teacher. Am I too old?

Man on phone: No, there's no maximum age.

*

I found myself telling him I wanted to teach maths. I had no desire to be an English teacher like Mum – a lifetime of writing meant I'd had it with words and their slippery ambiguity. What I felt I wanted was the certainty of numbers, and as maths was my favourite subject at school it seemed like a good choice. The man on the phone assured me I could teach maths without a degree in it, and that he could help me apply.

I hung up feeling light-headed. Maybe I'll actually do this, I thought.

The weekend after Dad's funeral I walked around the local park with Stan. Tentatively, I put the idea to him, expecting him to laugh. I thought he would remind me of how I used to 'help' him with his maths homework – when he couldn't see that there were 540 degrees in a pentagon, I flew into such a rage I sometimes made him cry.

But when I told him I was toying with the idea of leaving the *FT* and becoming a maths teacher he showed no surprise.

'Do it,' he said. 'Great idea.'

Not only was there no red light, but here was a young policeman in white gloves standing by the green light waving me through.

'Do you think I'd be able to do it?' I asked him. 'Could I be patient enough?'

'Don't see why not. You wouldn't shout at your pupils, because they wouldn't be your children.'

In the next few weeks I tried the idea out on everyone I met. Half thought it a splendid plan, half did not.

Gideon Rachman, my friend and fellow columnist at the *FT*, leaned back in his chair and did what I'd expected Stan to do when I told him my plan. He laughed.

'Let me get this straight,' he said. 'You'd be leaving a job that is well paid, that you're good at, that is glamorous and flexible – for something badly paid with low status that you'd probably be rubbish at.'

I remember looking at him sitting complacently in his chair in his office with its view of the Thames and thinking: You may be happy in your gilded cage but the door of mine has unexpectedly sprung open and I'm getting out.

It did occur to me at that point that I hadn't set foot in a classroom since I was in one myself in 1977 and that it might be wise to do some research before committing myself. One of my colleagues told me that his wife had also become a maths teacher late in life after a career in the City, and so I emailed her and invited myself to visit the West London comprehensive where she taught.

What's it like, I asked her over fish and chips in the school canteen. She said she was up until 11pm every night studying to stay ahead of her A level further maths class. When I asked if she missed the money, she said she'd solved that problem by never opening her pay slip.

Instead of being put off by the prospect of too much work for too little pay, I was inspired. I loved the adrenaline and bells between lessons and the corridors filled with jostling kids. Most of all I was impressed by her confident authority telling off a student who was loafing around outside the toilets. I could, just about, see myself doing that.

A few weeks later I went to see Lionel Barber, my editor at the *FT*. We'd started together at the paper the same week in April 1985 and had been colleagues for over three decades. He listened dumbfounded to what I had to say and warned against taking decisions when bereaved: I was too upset to be thinking straight. I said that on the contrary, being bereaved made me see things as they were and gave me a restless energy which I needed to capitalise on. Was I sure? he asked.

Yes, I replied, I was absolutely sure.

He then said he quite understood the need to give something back, which was why he had agreed to become chair of Tate. He said he could put in a word to help me get something a bit like that. I said it was a kind offer, but that wasn't the sort of being useful I was after.

In November 2016, I wrote a column telling readers I was quitting the following summer. The Sunday morning before my story was due to appear I was in the kitchen making coffee and looked at my phone to see I'd been scooped on my own news story (which was appropriate, as I don't think I was ever first with a story in my life) by Roy Greenslade in the *Guardian*.

LUCY KELLAWAY TO LEAVE THE FINANCIAL TIMES TO BECOME A TEACHER, said the headline. I read it – and started to cry.

This was an extraordinary response, given that the news was not exactly a surprise. It was as if, in the frantic excitement of preparing for my new working life, it hadn't occurred to me I was actually leaving my old one. This was not the first time I'd been so monumentally slow on the uptake. When I was pregnant with my first child I passed nine months obsessed with the thought of the birth itself, and it wasn't until lying comfortably in a hospital bed, numb with epidural and almost fully dilated, that the thought occurred to me: My, God, I'm going to have a baby!

I stood by the orange counter in my dressing gown, convulsed in sobs. I had done something irrevocable. As I howled, I read the story and then the comments underneath.

The first said: 'A loathsome PR stunt from the patronising corporate class. Teaching is not like running an artisan bakery in Shoreditch.'

The second: 'Good luck. Journalism into teaching. What could possibly go wrong? I look forward to her article "Why I left teaching" in two years.'

I stopped crying at once. Damn you, I thought, pulling myself together. I will show you.

However hard teaching was going to be, I reflected, it must be easier than running an artisan bakery as you don't have to get up at 4am and there isn't an 80 per cent chance you'll go bust and lose all your money.

Not all comments were quite so hostile, but everyone seemed agreed on one thing: this woman does not know what she's letting herself in for.

On that point, at least, they could not have been more right.

3

Teach Last

On an overcast evening in June 2016, less than a fortnight after Dad's funeral and a year before I finally left the *FT*, I went to the Chelsea Physic Garden's annual drinks party. The beauty of this event is you don't have to talk to anyone. You can wander around inspecting plants with a glass of Prosecco in one hand and a puff pastry canapé in the other, ignoring the great and the good who stand in linen suits and floral dresses on the lawn. I thought the evening might be a brief respite from grief – I did not expect it to change my life and set me on a rickety path towards the giddiest excitement that work has ever brought me.

I had been hiding in the medicinal plants section and had ventured out to get a refill when I was collared by a woman who looked familiar. She was Caroline Waldegrave, the cook, whom I'd interviewed many years earlier and liked so much I'd forgotten to ask any penetrating questions – so the resulting article did credit to neither of us.

We started talking and I found myself, like the Ancient Mariner, telling my story. I told her my father had just died and I was tired of writing and of interviewing people and was planning to become a maths teacher.

She nodded encouragingly so I expanded on the theme. I said that though there was no age limit to becoming a teacher the process of applying was off-putting to people my age – which made no sense, given the shortage of teachers. If there was a Teach First to scoop up bright graduates and turn them into teachers before they swanned off to McKinsey and Goldman Sachs, I went on, where was Teach Last for people like me at the other end of their careers, who had been in the civil service and McKinsey and now wanted to be more useful?

Caroline continued to listen and nod, as if all this made perfect sense. Then she told me her daughter, Katie Waldegrave, had been a teacher with Teach First and had then launched First Story, a charity that gets writers into schools. She was at home having just had twins and would be happy to talk to me.

I don't think I would have followed it up – I'd had at least four glasses of Prosecco and was mainly just holding forth. Becoming a teacher was enough of a challenge as it was and there was no way I was going to set up an organisation to help others do the same thing – I just liked talking about it. But the next day I got a message from Katie and so I left the office early and went to see her.

The woman who opened the door of the house in Shepherd's Bush seemed unusually perky for someone with ten-week-old babies, who she told me she'd just taken swimming. She handed me one infant and as she started to feed the other I told her about my half-baked idea. How many people was I looking for, she asked? Which subjects would they teach? How would I train them? To each question I said: I don't know, I haven't thought about it. All I know is that I want to be a teacher. I am sure there are people out there of roughly my age who want to do it too.

We talked for three hours, at the end of which I ran across the green to the Tube – not because I was in a hurry but because I was propelled by a strange elation I'd never felt before. Clearly the whole thing was crazy. I had been a wage slave all my life and had never shown the slightest entrepreneurial leaning, in fact had always felt mild horror when anyone said they wanted to start their own business. I'd watched David work around the clock establishing *Prospect*, and had lived through the insecurity, the worries about money, the fights with funders, the bone-crushing fatigue. I'd always thought: No thanks.

But now, out of the blue, here was an unlooked-for chance of starting something from scratch and I found myself thinking: Yes, why not? I didn't have a clue how to go about it, but that was part of the draw. What did I have to lose?

That evening I sent Katie an email:

Would you like to set up Teach Last with me? I'd love working with you. Please say yes.

*

Minutes later she replied:

> Oh my goodness but this is the nicest and most exciting
> email I've ever received. I've so many ideas and so many
> questions I want to put to people. Right this second I have
> to feed babies. Will respond in more sensible way later.

This is not how you are meant to choose a business partner.
The standard advice for people launching start-ups is to do due
diligence, check for complementary skills, and ensure the other
person has the time for what will be a bottomless pit of effort.

Katie had no noticeable spare time and neither did I as I
was proposing to continue working for the *FT* for another
year until I started in the classroom as I needed the money.
Also, our skills weren't remotely complementary. One meeting was enough to show that both of us liked talking about
ideas – or about anything at all – very fast and at the same
time. Both of us were enthusiasts. Both well connected. Neither noticeably interested in detail.

I wasn't worried about any of that. I liked talking to Katie
and I trusted her. My gut said yes, and it seemed to me then
the only part of me that counted.

At our next meeting we agreed what our roles would be.
She would run Teach Last as I had no useful experience and
anyway was still at the *FT*. I would be the non-executive
sounding board, chief publicist, flag waver, joint strategist,

fund raiser, general agitator and dogsbody. Katie would do everything else.

A week later I'm in Primrose Hill sitting in Lynda Gratton's garden. The London Business School professor is in a floaty dress, the jasmine is in bloom, and she has made a jug of strong coffee.

It's all very fragrant, but I'm feeling put out. Katie and I have decided to spend two weeks canvassing views and support from anyone we can think of who might be able to give us contacts, ideas or money. I've come to see Lynda because she has just co-written a book called *The 100-Year Life* and I know she is going to adore the idea of Teach Last. But when I explain I'm looking for people at the end of a conventional career who want to do something exhausting in their second half-century, she frowns.

> Lynda: I can see why people might want to visit schools to give a talk, but isn't what you're asking a bit of a commitment?
> Me: But there are so many people my age who are sick to the back teeth of their jobs.
> Lynda: Hmm. I don't think all people our age are fed up with their jobs. My fiancé [a hot-shot corporate lawyer] loves his work more than ever.

*

Feeling dashed, I cycle off to meet Katie, who has arranged for us to visit an academy school in West London in the middle of a housing estate. So far, we have decided to concentrate our efforts where we will have most impact, which means we will focus on finding trainees in maths, science and languages, where the shortage of teachers is most acute. We have also decided we will only work in schools with high levels of deprivation. This seems like the right thing to do – if our candidates want to become teachers in order to be useful, they will be more so in a challenging school than they would be in a private one. We sit in the office of its head teacher – a pugnacious man who looks barely 40 – and Katie explains what we are doing. He nods politely and says it's an interesting idea, but teacher training is exhausting for people in their 20s and frankly he can't see how people in their 50s would be able to manage it.

I tell him I'm 57 and ask if he finds me lacking in energy. He looks briefly embarrassed and assures me that not everyone is like me. I want to tell him what he's said is ageist and probably illegal, but I keep my mouth shut. I have the sense that keeping quiet is a skill I'm going to have to get better at.

The next day we go and see Teach First. The *FT*'s education correspondent has put me in touch with its head of external affairs, who used to work at the BBC. I email him, telling him what we are doing, and ask for a meeting. It occurs to me that though I'm nearly 60 I have never asked anyone for a meeting before to discuss a plan. It's not what journalists do and the novelty is thrilling.

We have high hopes that Teach First will be so taken with the idea of Teach Last they'll want to do it in partnership with us. We have it all planned out – they will do all the logistical stuff as they have a huge back office and know how to train teachers, and we will set about doing the fun bit of finding prospective teachers. We sit in the Teach First canteen with two of their top executives who lean back in their chairs looking sceptical. They say they've considered a scheme like this in the past, but rejected it as persuading older people to be teachers is too difficult.

Teach Last might have ended there, had it not been for my friend Lucy Heller. Lucy, who helped me through Oxford when I was miserable and threatening to leave, and then carried me through the collapse of my marriage, comes to the rescue again. Now she has more than sympathy to offer as she happens to run ARK, one of the biggest chains of academy schools. When I first floated the idea of becoming a teacher to her, Lucy didn't laugh. Forty years ago, she was taught English by my mum and understands not just my 50-something ennui but the family pull. When I told her about Teach Last, she saw what I saw: the gap in the market, and the strength in a marketing campaign led by someone – me – who was practising what she preached and becoming a teacher herself.

Early on, Katie and I go for a meeting with Lucy at her office on Kingsway. It feels a bit weird to be facing your best friend so formally across her boardroom table, but Lucy listens to our plans seriously, and then says our teachers could be trained by ARK and teach in ARK schools, all of which are in deprived areas. Better still, she says her charity will 'incubate' ours, which means we can get to work at once, and exist under ARK's legal umbrella until we sort ourselves out and become an independent charity.

'Thank you,' we say.

Outside Katie and I hug each other in the street. We're in business.

During those early months our spirits soar and crash. One minute the idea is total rubbish, bound to be a disaster. The next minute it is sheer genius.

In my most deflated times I think Teach Last will hardly find any candidates and they will all turn out to be useless at teaching.

'What is the smallest number of teachers we can launch with,' I ask Katie on a particularly gloomy day. 'Eight,' she replies.

In my most inflated moments I see Teach Last helping to fill the national shortage of teachers with an endless supply of older recruits, bursting with life experience, changing the look of every staffroom in the country. More than that, I see us overturning the ridiculously outdated way people my age have been taught to view their careers – you do one thing until you retire, after which you either play golf or construct a portfolio of a bit of this and a bit of that. We will show that it is possible, desirable and perfectly natural for people to start again in their 50s – not just as teachers but as anything at all. When the journalist Sarah Sands hears about Teach Last she says she's going to trump it by launching Nurse Last and becoming its aging standard bearer. She's joking, but it strikes me as a great idea. I wish someone else would do it.

By September, Katie has drawn up a business plan which commits us to finding 20 oldish professionals in our first year and supporting them through teacher training provided by ARK. On the strength of it we go, cap in hand, to the Department for Education in the hope of getting some public money. The two of us sit in a room with a taciturn civil servant and talk excitedly, waving our arms and interrupting each other. The woman is not impressed. She will follow our progress with interest, she says, committing the public purse to not a single sausage.

So far we have no funds at all. I have emailed every rich person I have ever met – all the bankers and hedge-fund people I came across for 30 years on the *FT.* I get lots of polite replies but nothing doing.

Despite the rejections, I find I quite like asking for money. This is a surprise given that it took me more than two decades as an employee to pluck up the courage to ask for a pay rise. But now that the money is not for me but for my fledgling charity, I've stopped being a wallflower and become gleefully brazen. Please give us money, I say to anyone who I think has any to spare – and this is what we'd do with it.

I approach Winton, the hedge fund run by David Harding, who is interested in maths education and has paid for the handsome mathematics gallery at the Science Museum, designed by Zaha Hadid. I met him a couple of years earlier and bonded over a shared loathing of business bullshit – which means I have no qualms emailing him out of the blue and asking for cash. Would he like to give us some money to help us find some maths teachers? Miraculously, generously, he says he would – and offers us enough money to cover our entire first year of operating.

That week we seemed to be on a roll. Katie took me to see Charlotte Hogg (who chaired Katie's first charity) in her marbled office at the Bank of England, where she was then Chief Operating Officer. Charlotte sat there in her leather jacket, wired for action, nodding incisively and agreeing not only to chair Teach Last but also to find us a top lawyer and accountant to join us on the board.

Afterwards, I walked out into Threadneedle Street, just a few yards from the old J.P. Morgan offices where my 22-year-old self used to cry in the loo. I marvelled at how easy this very hard thing was turning out to be and what a difference a few contacts seemed to be making – without the people Katie and I knew between us, I doubt if we would have managed to get our idea off the ground. But as it was, Charlotte Hogg believed we could do this when we barely believed it ourselves because she knew and trusted Katie. She also seemed to trust me on the strength of having read my column all those years – which was a bit rum as writing a sarky column and starting a social enterprise have precisely nothing in common.

Three months after my first meeting with Katie, we have a launch date (early November) but don't yet have a website or even a name. Katie has never liked Teach Last as she says it makes it sound like the crematorium is the next stop, but I am wedded to it as it's both accurate and funny. We email everyone we know for suggestions – the upshot of which is Teach Last is out, to be replaced by the workaday name of Now Teach. I don't love it but I don't hate it either: it is perfectly inoffensive.

Only it turns out to cause so much offence in one quarter that our launch has to be delayed. Some years earlier Teach First registered the name Teach Now (which they aren't using) and object to our name for being too similar to theirs. Their lawyers then have to talk to our lawyers (whom Katie has persuaded to work for us for nothing). The upshot, after several interminable conference calls, which are so frustrating I have to spring onto the orange counter at home and take it out on the cobwebs above with a broom handle, is that we get to keep our so-so name. The skirmish is ridiculous, but I'm pinching myself. How come Teach First want our name when we don't even exist? Is it because they fear that one day we'll be massive?

On 21 November we launch. My article is live on the *FT* website announcing that I'm leaving the *FT* and inviting people to come with me. I wake before dawn and look at my phone. My inbox is a sea of bold unread messages, page upon page of them. The first has a subject that says BRAVO, which is one of my all-time favourite subject lines in messages from readers. The second I'm rather less keen on, though spookily it differs from the first by just one letter: BRAVE. I don't like being called brave, because whenever people accuse me of it – 'that was a brave column to write' – they generally don't mean it as a compliment. In any case, right now brave is the last thing I am. I am euphoric, so high on excitement I'm not aware of any risk at all.

I get on my bike while it's still dark and cycle to Broadcasting House. I've convinced the editor of BBC's *Today* that the birth of Now Teach is sufficiently newsworthy for a spot on the country's most prestigious news programme. I'm up against John Humphrys, the fearsome interviewer, but once on air I feel I'm smashing it: I'm fielding his hostile questions, urging all middle-aged bankers to follow me into the classroom; I'm being humble and funny. Just now I've watched the clip online and seen a four-year-younger version of myself, gabbling, red-eyed and manic. I appear possessed with a mad, religious fervour. I wouldn't follow me anywhere.

Still, the message resonated. I accepted every other media gig that came my way, saying the same thing again and again. The story acquired legs and by the middle of the week Rabbi Lord Jonathan Sacks used Now Teach as a peg for his *Thought for the Day* slot on Radio 4, in which he spotted a hitherto unremarked-upon similarity between me and Moses, who also changed his career late in the day from leading the Israelites to becoming a teacher.

In the first few weeks we were contacted by half a dozen TV documentary makers wanting to film our ex-lawyers and ex-derivatives traders as they hit the classroom. When the first producer got in touch, I phoned Katie, almost levitating with glee. She pointed out that the nature of their interest was not likely to be friendly. Who would want to commission a programme about a humble ex-banker becoming a jolly good maths teacher? It was risky enough starting Now Teach when we didn't know what we were doing; to do it under the glare of a TV camera would have been insane.

She was, as usual, right. While we had become, briefly, a national news story, behind the scenes there was not much more than me and Katie, two laptops, a generous donor and an agreement with ARK. That was about it.

*

On the day of the launch I go straight from the BBC to the ARK canteen, the closest thing Now Teach has to an office. Katie is on the phone trying to buy more server space as the website has crashed, and next to her is a young woman I haven't met, who has been more or less pulled off the street to help us. Rebecca has chaotic black hair and is bent over her laptop getting the details of the applicants off the website and onto a spreadsheet.

Me: How many people have applied?
Rebecca (not looking up from her work): A few hundred.
Me: Christ.

I roll up my sleeves to start ringing the people who have registered an interest but my mobile is out of battery and I can't work out who I'm meant to be calling because, despite 36 years in the workforce, I've never used a spreadsheet. Rebecca, evidently not cowed by her new boss, starts to laugh. When she regains the ability to speak, she shows me what to do, and then goes off to borrow a charger. How is it possible, I wonder, to feel both omnipotent and impotent – both at the same time?

The first candidate I call turns out to be a former CEO of an asset management company with a degree in maths from Cambridge. I tell him about our application process, which Katie has drawn up on the back of an envelope, and he sounds very keen.

The next day I get an email from him saying he has discussed his plan with his wife over dinner, and she reminded him that he didn't like children very much so, on reflection and with apologies, he was withdrawing his application.

He's not alone – many of those early applicants are over-excited fantasists who haven't thought it through. But it doesn't matter – there are enough others who seem genuinely promising. And every successive article I write brings still more.

Whenever we have a pause, Katie and I look over the applicants and gloat. To be so profoundly right about something feels like nothing else on earth. We were sure these people were out there – and here they bloody well are.

The scale of the publicity has an effect on the government, bringing on a change of heart. Soon after the launch, we are summoned to see Nick Gibb, the Minister of State for School Standards. This time, we vow we not to talk over each other or wave our arms, and Katie has prepared figures and slides to back us up. We sit anxiously at one end of an empty wood-panelled committee room waiting for the minister who comes in late, beaming. Gibb is a year younger than me, and gets it. Teacher shortage is one of his biggest problems – and we could be part of an answer. He flips through the slides, but he seems to have already made up his mind.

'Find these people some money,' he instructs his minions. They nod, though I fancy their teeth are gritted.

The schools minister might have been on board, but many weren't. In the week after our launch I got an email from a former journalist who'd quit in her early 50s to retrain as a teacher and found the whole experience so harrowing she quit after a term and has not had a paid job since. She accused me of being a Pied Piper – leading innocent bankers and lawyers to their certain deaths in the classroom.

'Wait until you have experienced school life for a while, before you encourage others into the risk,' she warned.

I should have been shaken by this. Acts of hubris don't come much bigger than what I was doing yet at the time I refused to consider whether she might be right. Instead I wrote back politely assuring her that most of our teachers were working in ARK schools, which were well run, and that we had warned everyone that training was going to be murderously hard. And in any case, weren't they adults, well able to take their own decisions?

There was another reason I didn't let this Cassandra get to me – I was simply too busy. Getting applications might have been easier than we'd ever thought, but picking the right people was turning into a nightmare.

As most Now Teachers were to be trained by ARK, they had to go through the same application process as regular 20-something applicants – which I assumed they would find a doddle. I remember sitting in on the assessment of a former KPMG partner in his late 50s, who had a loud, posh voice and a swagger in his step and was being interviewed by an ARK employee in her 20s.

Interviewer: Can you tell me about a time when you received negative feedback?

KPMG partner: Gosh! That's a hard one. It's usually
me giving the feedback!

Interviewer: It doesn't need to be recent.

KPMG partner: I don't think I can. (*pause*) Well, I suppose
I get negative feedback from my children! Will that do?

He scored abysmally, failing to give any evidence he had any of
the dratted 'competencies' – including moral purpose, humility
and ability to learn from feedback – deemed necessary to
become a good teacher. ARK said they didn't want him; I was
furious. I reasoned he was an alpha male who hated failing at
things and so would make it his business to succeed as a teacher.

The next candidate was a woman who was then something
important at the Foreign Office and now was applying to
teach languages.

Interviewer: Can you tell me about a time when you
were involved in a stressful situation?

Negotiator: Well, when I was negotiating for the release
of hostages – that was stressful.

Interviewer: What strategies did you use to cope with
your levels of stress on that occasion?

Negotiator: We were trying to get British citizens out
alive, so my levels of stress weren't really the issue.

Interviewer: But you must have had some techniques
for reducing your stress?

Negotiator: I don't think so. This really wasn't about me.

She also failed this part of the process, deemed insufficiently resilient. This caused another row with ARK.

> Interviewer: I could only give her a 2 on resilience because she didn't have any strategies for helping deal with stress.
>
> Me (*voice raised*): Oh, for God's sake! She does one of the most stressful jobs on earth, is still alive, looks healthy and calm. What more evidence do you need that she is bloody resilient? What did you want – for her to tell you she burned a scented candle to calm down?!

Looking back on it I feel guilty about how vicious I was to these young women in my attempt to get my candidates through. Though even if I'd been more moderate, disagreement was inevitable. As I saw it, the interviewers did not understand successful people in their 50s. As they saw it, I didn't have the first idea what it took to be a teacher or just how stressful the five-day-a-week onslaught was going to be, even for people who had done high-pressure jobs. Both of us were on to something – but neither was yet ready to admit the other had a leg to stand on.

In the end we agreed on 45 candidates: twice as many as in our business plan and each one, superficially at least, more than twice as impressive as I'd hoped for. There was someone who used to work in the media, a former NASA physicist and the ex-head of a hospital trust. There were plenty of lawyers and bankers. The oldest was 71. The youngest was 42.

They were a varied lot, with fewer common denominators than I'd expected. Not all were fed up with their old jobs – quite a few still loved their work, but wanted a change. Quite a few were already retired – but found that they hated having so little to do. A few had made proper fortunes – one man who had worked in the City let slip he was taking a 98 per cent pay cut to be a teacher – but for others money was more of a problem. One candidate borrowed money from his aged father and another took out a second mortgage on his house. There were only two things we had in common: we wanted to be useful and we wanted to do something new.

In August 2017, just two weeks before our first brush with the classroom, I invite all 45 Now Teachers to a celebratory supper at my house.

I stand on the table in the garden and survey their expectant faces. I say – and mean it from the heart – that this is the proudest moment of my professional life. I then remind them of what I've said from the beginning: quitting isn't an option. Being a teacher isn't like getting a job at PwC – for the sake of our pupils, I say, we have a moral duty to stick it out at least until the end of the year, no matter how hard the going gets. We must prove to all the sceptics that we, an aged bunch of slightly weird professionals, are just as good at teaching as 22-year-olds. I said this with such ferocity that if anyone disagreed they didn't let on – which led me to conclude the message was deemed reasonable and had been fully understood.

Later that evening, Peter Jerrom, who used to trade foreign exchange and is going to teach maths, sidles up to me clutching his drink, very much the wheeler dealer. He wants to bet on how many of the 45 will find teacher training too hard and drop out before we qualify.

Me: Two. Maximum.
Peter (*puffing out his cheeks in disbelief*): That's way too low. Twelve.
Me (*indignant*): Way too high.

We shake hands on it.

I have conveniently forgotten the financial terms of this bet. But Peter, who is now a formidable maths teacher and head of Sixth Form at his school, often likes to remind me I owe him a good deal of money.

4

Wrench

The phone rings on my empty desk. It's Martin, the man on Reception who has said hello to me every morning and good-bye every evening for the best part of three decades. If you count the minor smiles and nods at lunchtime as I've popped out for a sandwich, we must have acknowledged each other a total of 60,000 times.

'Hello, Luce,' Martin is saying. 'I've got a visitor for you.'

I get up and walk through the Features department to the front desk. I pass Andrew, a fellow columnist and *FT* lifer who is peering through his glasses at his screen and typing with intent. I pass Sebastian, a young, irrepressible political reporter, who is shouting down the phone to some contact. I pass Isobel, who is silently editing copy. To all of them this is a normal day.

In Reception a man with a hairy mic and a shoulder bag full of recording equipment waits for me. I receive his hug but am not entirely pleased to see him. He is making a radio documentary about me retraining as a teacher and has persuaded me that it would be great to record my last day at the *Financial Times* for a bit of contrast.

I take him back to my desk, a grey melamine rectangle with a view onto a pebbled flat roof. It is where I've sat day in, day out since the early 1990s, carrying out the activities of my working life: sending emails to people sitting ten yards away, wasting time on Twitter, bidding for things on eBay as well as doing what I was paid to do – write columns. I look at the ergonomic office chair covered in food stains from years of eating at my desk. It occurs to me I've spent more time in contact with this piece of furniture than any other in my entire life – with the exception of my bed.

The producer turns his recorder on.

'Can you explain that today is your last day and describe how you feel?'

I say it's a momentous day – to be leaving after 32 years – and though I feel sad, I've had a great run and it's the right time to hang up my hat and move on. I say I need to get out of my comfort zone, but then stop myself, remembering a sneery column I once wrote on the stupidity of anyone who professed any desire to leave a comfort zone, which is by definition comfortable, and therefore irrefutably better than anything less so.

None of my clichés will make it into the documentary – possibly the producer is bored by them or maybe he knows them to be lies.

How I'm actually feeling is sick, frightened and sad. I am poor at ending relationships, but now, arbitrarily, when there is so much that is still good about my relationship with the *Financial Times*, I'm terminating it. I am leaving behind lots of people I like, as well as a set of habits that has given order to my life. My days have been measured out, if not in coffee spoons, then in trips up to the canteen, visits to the vending machine for Diet Cokes and KitKats, and untold hours spent chatting to my columnist friends. I have no idea what life will be like without all this. The office and this job have given me solace and structure when I was hardly coping – when my marriage was falling apart and when my mum died. The *FT* has been so much a part of me, in my very bone marrow, it seems unlikely that when I come out the other side I'll be the same person.

When I joined the paper in April 1985 I was a round-faced, insecure, hard-working 26-year-old in a cardigan I'd knitted myself. In the years that followed, the *FT* provided me with not just a job, but identity, status, stimulation, friends – and even a husband. Within my first hour there, I'd set eyes on the lanky man I was going to marry and have four children with, so on the *Sliding Doors* view of history, if I had not got that job writing company reports, almost every part of my life would have turned out differently and, almost certainly, worse.

I joined the *FT* in the golden era of offices, in the days before political correctness and health and safety – it was a time of cast-iron typewriters, tea ladies, canteens selling spotted dick, and office pranks. In the early days I remember writing a critical article about a company and coming in the next morning to find its irate CEO on the telephone. Only it turned out not to be the CEO but 29-year-old David Goodhart, a fellow reporter, calling from the other side of the newsroom – much to the amusement of those who sat around him. In time I forgave him – in fact I came to see it as so funny that I married him.

One of the things I liked best about my office life is it provided me with a different way of being. I had two selves, a home self who was badly dressed, un-made-up, harassed and inclined to shout, and a work self who was slightly better dressed, wore mascara, was even-tempered and, on a good day, witty. I remember taking Arty to visit the *FT* when he was at primary school, and one of my colleagues said to him, 'Your mother is so funny.' My son frowned. 'No, she's not,' he replied. Later he said to me, 'I don't think I've ever seen you laugh.'

The biggest and oddest difference between the two selves was my approach to clutter – at home I outlawed it, while my desk at work resembled the yard of Steptoe and Son. Today I can see its smooth surface, which I last saw on the day I claimed it, decades earlier. I've just had a mad fit of draconian clearing that even Marie Kondo might have judged extreme, in the course of which I swept my entire professional life into the bin. The old piles of magazines and newspapers, ancient letters from readers, empty wrappers from my favourite cheese-and-ham toasties, an unfeasibly large number of pens and pencils, half-full spiral notebooks, chargers to BlackBerrys I no longer own, books that might contain future column ideas: three decades of office detritus is now in the big metal recycling drum by my desk. I hesitated only over a few hideous awards trophies – not over whether to keep them, but whether they belonged in the recycling or in general rubbish.

Pre clear-out the junk was piled high. Post clear-out I have nothing physical to show for 32 years as a journalist, or rather nothing from the last 25. Until the mid-1990s we had secretaries whose job it was to cut out every article each journalist wrote and stick them into big red scrapbooks, two of which are at home and have survived all purges. Back then everything seemed more permanent: the newspaper was printed on hot metal presses in the basement of the office; every night on the way home I'd walk through the print room and smell the ink on the presses that were cranking into action.

The producer is asking me what has changed at the *FT* in the time I've worked there. The answer is everything and nothing. The way news is produced and the way people consume it has changed beyond measure, but the actual job of a journalist – finding things out and writing stories readers want to read – is pretty much the same as when I started out.

One thing that has changed is how we rate ourselves, and how the paper rates us. In the old days we knew if an article was any good because people would come up to us and say they liked it. Now, thanks to a dastardly bit of software called Lantern, journalists have immediate, real-time feedback on how their pieces are doing online. For each article you can track the number of hits, shares, comments – as well as how long readers spent on the page. Worse, you can compare this data with any other article – which allowed us to spend our days surreptitiously logging into Lantern to monitor our (un) popularity relative to that of our colleagues. It was as addictive as Instagram: a tool that would allow us to feel awful any time, at the drop of a hat.

The producer is asking if there is one article I've written I feel most proud of. In preparation for this question, I've being poring over my life's work and have made an odd discovery. The pieces I remember thinking were brilliant at the time now strike me as so-so – while the ones I struggled with are less awful than I'd remembered. Overall, most of the articles strike me now as much-of-a-muchness, broadly OK, if a bit dated. The whole exercise was a downer, in that I couldn't stop myself wondering what, taken together, all these thousands of articles amounted to.

The red scrapbook is full of technical news stories from the early days, including an impressively niche one on agricultural equipment manufacturers, in which I painstakingly explain the superiority of the square baler over the round one. There are many more from my stint in Brussels where I was posted in 1990 to cover the impending single market. I wrote faithful stories about new European legislation in semiconductors and sausage meat, leaving my counterpart on the *Telegraph*, Boris Johnson, to whip up his own faithless scoops: Brussels bans the British banger. I am proud of my reporting as I worked so hard trying to understand the legal detail – so much so that I felt personal outrage over Brexit (on top of all the other outrage) as it meant all that effort had been a total waste of time.

Then there are a full 23 years' worth of weekly columns, which I started writing in 1994 when I was pregnant with Arty. Someone had had the idea of jollying up the newsless Monday paper with a lighter column on work, and as I'd already shown aptitude at what the paper ploddingly liked to call 'taking a sideways look' at something, I was the obvious person for the job. If I knew then I'd go on writing this column as Arty grew from baby, to child, to teenager and to grown man, I would have been horrified. But Monday after Monday, that's what happened. If you take into account six weeks' holiday a year, one final maternity leave and three four-week sabbaticals, I must have written a total of 1,023 columns.

That is an awful lot of ideas, even if you allow for the fact that, like most columnists, I was never frightened of repeating myself. It is also a huge amount of effort: whether the idea was new or recycled I sweated and agonised, drafted and re-drafted before finally submitting the piece to the page editor with the uncertain feeling: Will this do?

The process of column writing was like beating egg whites. I'd start with something yellowish and slimy and get to work with a whisk. Sometimes I would get the words to stand up in stiff white peaks and sometimes they'd collapse. Though even this was subjective: the columns I liked were seldom the ones that readers did. What they seemed to enjoy most were the endless columns mocking business bullshit, against which I waged a remarkably unsuccessful 25-year campaign. While I was busy preaching to the converted, the unconverted went on to commit ever-greater atrocities. There is an article from the early 1990s in which I rail against the mathematically non-sensical phrase '110 per cent committed'; in my final piece on the subject 25 years later, I sadly note how much more bullshitty bullshit had become with this quote from a manager on LinkedIn: 'We are focused 1,000,000 per cent on positive, move forward, actionable efforts to help facilitate change.'

At some point in the 1990s, when Dilbert and Bridget Jones were the funniest things in newspapers, I set about creating the *FT*'s own version to be a rip-off amalgam of the two. I came up with Martin Lukes, a jargon-spewing, back-stabbing manager. Every week I'd write a column consisting of the emails he sent to his colleagues at the fictional AB Global where he was Director of Special Projects. Some readers hated the column from the start, others were baffled as to why a random manager's emails were appearing in the paper. By the time they saw the joke, I'd got sick of the company of this tiresome man, who contained the worst parts of my male colleagues, my husband and all the businessmen I'd ever come across. This was the low point of my career: there is little worse than writing comedy that you know (and everyone else knows) is no longer funny. Inspiration only returned when it came to thinking up the perfect way for Martin Lukes to die. In a rare flash of insight, I knew he must meet his death in a teambuilding accident. I had him jumping out of a plane, only he was too busy sending self-promotional tweets as he fell to pull the cord on his parachute. Was this final Lukes column the best thing I'd written? Out of time and out of context it seems laboured and unfunny – you had to be there.

I briefly considered picking one of the hundreds of interviews I've done over the years. There's one with Jonathan Franzen from 2015 that I was pleased with at the time, in which he moans about how horrid 1-per-centers are, and when I point out he is one himself, he explains: 'I'm a poor person who has money.' But as I read it again, I felt uneasy. I'd drawn Franzen as a vain, humourless, self-indulgent, doctrinaire pill. The piece was funny, but was it fair? Were any of my interviews fair?

As I wrote each one, I knew exactly what I needed to do: get the reader by the scruff of the neck and forcibly entertain them. Otherwise why would they be bothered to read about my meeting with Bear Grylls or Richard Gere or even the Archbishop of Canterbury? As it's easier to be funny when your subject is being vain, tiresome, illogical or downright mad, my strategy was always to invite them to show themselves to disadvantage – to give them enough rope to hang themselves.

All my subjects were accomplished people and they generally turned out to be adept with a noose, given the right encouragement. Franzen put his head straight into his with no prodding from me, but now I think about it, I wonder if it was right to let him. Wouldn't it have been better to have taken the rope out of his hands and see what he had to say without it?

After some humming and hawing I finally settle on an article I wrote about the absurd ritual of dinner parties 15 years earlier, which produced a large mailbag. Back then I had four youngish children and was often invited to dinner at other people's houses. Invariably the host had been slaving all day over Nigella's clementine cake and the River Cafe's wet polenta with fresh porcini – which not only meant they were frazzled by the time guests arrived, but that much of the evening was devoted to discussing the food, which might have been nice to eat but was a dud as a conversational topic. Worst of all, it raised the culinary bar and made me scared to ask them back.

I wanted to prove it doesn't matter what you serve so long as the company is OK, the atmosphere relaxed and alcohol plentiful. So I invited over ten people who gave particularly fancy dinners themselves, and served a meal that took about ten minutes to make and consisted of all David's favourite dishes: Pringles, chicken Kievs with Uncle Ben's rice, followed by Viennetta. Afterwards, I sent out questionnaires apologising for having made guinea pigs of them and quizzed them on the food and the evening. The survey results were most encouraging: everyone claimed to have had a great time; most of the men loved the food, and only one guest said she was horrified by the menu, but added she'd been happy to eat nothing as she was on a diet anyway.

Now, as I continue my laboured explanation into the tape recorder of this long-ago article, I find I don't think it's funny anymore. I can't relate to it at all – or to the 45-year-old version of myself who wrote it. The dinner party is no longer a part of my life, and far from mocking food hysterics, I seem to have become one myself. These days I can make a Nigella clementine cake at the shake of a stick. I am even prepared to discuss an Ottolenghi recipe, so long as there are other things to talk about too.

So I retract my choice, and say that's the point about journalism. It's not meant to last. I don't need a favourite article of all time. I just need to comfort myself with the thought that over the years I wrote things that seemed good enough on the day they were published.

The producer turns off the recorder. It's 3.45 and it's time.

Downstairs I hover by the main news desk, the producer by my side. A message has gone out on everyone's email: 'Come and say goodbye to Lucy Kellaway in newsroom NOW' – but there is hardly anyone here. Like all journalists, my colleagues know the difference between an official deadline and a real one. I stand awkwardly and wait. I am joined by Mike Skapinker, my oldest *FT* friend and longest-serving office spouse, to whom I have spent thousands of hours chatting over the decades. But now, as he stands next to me in the newsroom, I can't think of a single thing to say to him. After a bit, colleagues start to drift in and the subeditors sitting in the newsroom step away from their screens and gather in a self-conscious horseshoe around me.

I've stood here at least a hundred times in the last 30 years and witnessed these spectacles from the other side. I always found them sticky, partly because they are so asymmetrical. To the person leaving this is a big deal, but to everyone else it's a blip. No matter how senior or well-liked the journalist is or how long they've worked there, the newspaper always gets along without them just fine. This thought – that I'm the only person who cares – is vaguely calming to me as I stand here, heart hammering.

The newsroom is almost full and Lionel Barber is now sauntering across the office, holding a piece of paper. He takes his place next to me.

'Lucy.' He starts portentously, his eyes moving between me and the audience. 'What can I say? Journalist. Columnist. Interviewer. Friend.'

I don't want to listen to this. I go through the first line of my own speech in my head to try to stay calm. He says a few things and the crowd is laughing – but I can't take in what he's saying. He turns to his sheet of paper and starts to read, very slowly and with a lot of random innuendo. At first I don't know what he's reading but then I recognise a column I wrote about ten years earlier, which he seems to think (wrongly) was written about him and is adding nudge-nudge emphasis in odd places. I long for this recitation to stop, and so, judging by their faces, do my colleagues.

He's finished at last and it's my turn. The huge furry mic is suspended on a long stick a foot from my mouth. I have no notes; I don't need them. I've said the words to myself over and over lying in the bath and riding my bike. I know what I'm going to say.

I tell them how a good friend of mine had unkindly pointed out to me the previous weekend that leaving the *FT* was obviously going to be traumatic for me as it was the most successful relationship of my life. It has lasted longer than with any of my children and longer than with my husband.

My colleagues laugh in a slightly uncomfortable way.

I go on to say that the *Financial Times* stands for three values, all of which I respect, even though I've failed to live up to the first two, and have exploited the third shamelessly.

The first is accuracy, which I admire with all my heart as I've found it so very hard to achieve myself. I once referred to someone as the 'late' so-and-so when (as his wife subsequently pointed out in a letter to the paper) he was still alive, if a little poorly. Once I made a mistake in a news story and managed to make a second, different, mistake in the subsequent correction.

The second value is the paper's high-mindedness, which I like even though I've spent my career dragging the newspaper downmarket. Martin Wolf, the newspaper's most serious columnist, accused me early on of running a one-woman campaign to turn the *FT* into the *Daily Star* after I wrote an article slagging off the dress sense of some of Britain's captains of industry.

The third is the most splendid of all. The *FT* has old-fashioned views about Church and State – we journalists can write whatever we like without worrying about who is paying our salaries. I tell them how one New Year the CEO of Pearson (which then owned the *FT*) sent a motivational email to the entire company saying: 'What gets me fired up is knowing that each of you come to work every day ready to do something miraculous.' I thought this so dim and far-fetched – a miracle per person, per day? – I cut and pasted her email and reprinted it, word for word, as the motivational New Year memo from Martin Lukes.

No one stopped me. Later, I heard through the grapevine that the Pearson boss didn't see the funny side, and even less so when the story was picked up by *Private Eye*, but she never let on to me.

The *FT* also seemed fine about my losing the paper millions of pounds. There was the time I made a passing swipe at Meg Whitman, CEO of Hewlett Packard, for having said something vacuous at Davos. The next day I got an email from her PR man saying that the *FT* 'should take more seriously its relationship with its advertisers before writing such things'. I set to and wrote a column about the man's menacing email, pointing out that, on the contrary, what made the *FT* such a great newspaper was that we never took into account this relationship before writing what we believed to be the truth. The result was millions in advertising down the drain. No one told me off. They congratulated me on having written a decent column.

I end by committing the ultimate no-no and try to poach my colleagues. Come with me, I say to the 200 or so familiar faces who stand facing me. Do something useful. (This has the excellent result that an *FT* picture editor is now a chemistry teacher at a North London comp.)

I'm almost done. I say that though I'm sad, I'm not going to cry because I know I'm doing the right thing. I'm sure I want to be a teacher, and this is the right time to go.

Everyone is clapping. My voice didn't break and there was no hesitation or deviation. I am still dry-eyed. But that isn't because I know I'm doing the right thing – it's because I'm having a colossal out-of-body experience, almost as big as the one I had when I gave the address at Dad's funeral. This is too much and I can't deal with it so have absented myself from proceedings altogether.

I'm handed a card and a mock-up of an *FT* front page with a hideous cartoon of me at a blackboard and a series of fake news stories my colleagues have written about me. There is a trolley with drinks on it. Once upon a time everyone would have had a few glasses of wine and taken another back to their desks at four in the afternoon. Now people have a quick orange juice before scurrying back to work. Some people are hugging me and saying nice things, but I want this bit to be over.

Followed by the hairy mic held high, I walk through the newsroom towards the door. The journalists are drumming their hands on the table: this 'banging out' is a throwback to the old days of hot metal when printers would thump their tools when anyone left as a sign of respect.

In Reception Martin enfolds me in his arms and says he has some farewell advice to give me from his son, who works in schools. 'Look out for any kids called Jordan – they're always trouble.'

I disentangle myself, promise to steer clear of all Jordans, and go out through the revolving doors for the last time.

'Take care, Luce,' he says, to my departing back.

This undoes me. I stand on Southwark Bridge and start to cry. I unlock my bike and put the mock-up front page and the card with everybody's signatures into my bike pannier. I will keep these. But I can't look at them. Not just yet.

That evening I will give a big party in my garden at home for *FT* colleagues past and present. David will come, and when the party is in full throttle, he will stand up on a plant pot, with his foot crushing one of the young stems, and propose a toast. I'll be slightly annoyed that he's still playing the patriarch in my house, and more annoyed that he's standing on my hydrangea, but mostly I'll be pleased he's here along with all the other people I've ever worked with.

An entire *This Is Your Life* of ex-colleagues will come through my house. My children will pass round drinks. I will drink and drink but be too wired to feel drunk. All I will say to anyone on an endless loop is: 'This is so weird.'

The next morning I will wake to a prodigious sense of relief. I am no longer at the *FT*, I am out the other side – and even though I will have a savage hangover, I will notice that I'm still entirely myself, and I will think (wrongly) that the hardest bit is over.

5

First Year

It is my first day at school and I am hiding in the staff toilet whispering into the recording app on my phone.

'There are no pupils in yet, thank God,' I'm saying. 'It's an inset day. But I'm lost. I don't how to get to the auditorium, where I'm meant to be right now.'

The recording is interrupted by a rattling of the door handle as someone tries to get in. I give up – I'll try again later. I have agreed to keep an audio diary of my first few days of teacher training for Radio 4 listeners, which seemed like great publicity for Now Teach when they asked me to do it but now is the last straw.

In the empty corridor I spot a teacher and ask the way to the auditorium. Follow me, she says. She breaks into a run, which I later learn is to avoid having the door shut in her face and be shamed for lateness in front of the entire teaching body. This is a departure from my old life, in which being on time for a meeting suggested you weren't busy or important enough.

Trotting along behind her I explain that I'm new.

'What subject?' she asks, and I say I'm a maths trainee. She turns to have another look at me. 'Wow,' she says. 'I'd assumed you were a governor or something.'

About 150 members of staff are already sitting in the auditorium waiting for the head teacher's welcome. Dotted among the sea of young heads are three old ones – bald, grey or both – attached to bodies wearing expensive City suits. These are my fellow Now Teach trainees, one of whom smiles and waves. I'd like to hug him.

'Welcome back!' the principal is saying. 'I hope you had a good rest.' So far, I'm with her, but thereafter there isn't a single thing she says that I understand. She's talking about GCSEs and something called Progress 8. She throws around the numbers 0.9 and 1.1, but I have no idea what they mean. She moves on to a discussion on pupil premium, which I do know means (roughly) free school meals. I also know that about half the school qualify, but I have no idea what the PP numbers on the board mean, coded in red and green. She then says there is a change to how teachers must input data for detentions on SIMS (isn't that a computer game my daughter used to play?), as well as a new one-way system for students walking around the school. I'm none the wiser.

For the benefit of the new staff she says the school is a 'gromp' – an old-fashioned grammar for comprehensive pupils. It is unashamedly strict, a well-oiled machine that provides an excellent education for all, and every year gets students into Oxbridge. Duly we see pictures of the five students who made it last year, three of whom, I note, are Black.

Hackney is one of the poorest boroughs in London, just behind Newham and Tower Hamlets. It has more adults with no qualifications than anywhere else in the city and only a third of the population is white British. This school was once one of the worst schools in the country until it was shut down in the mid-1990s and reopened as one of the country's first academies. What this new incarnation has achieved is remarkable. How it has achieved it is more controversial.

'Here, we like to talk about positive fear,' the principal is saying.

I sit and listen, a tingle of anxiety passing down my spine. I survey the auditorium and look at the faces of the young teachers. I don't think I've ever felt as out of my depth. On my first day at the *Investors Chronicle* in 1984 I was told to write an article about the gilt market and I remember the despair I felt as I knew neither what a gilt was nor how to write an article. That now seems like child's play. Soon I will face a live audience of teenagers and I still have no idea how to teach, what to teach, when to teach or who I'll be teaching. I don't even know how to turn the classroom lights on.

Liam, the tracksuited head of PE who is also in charge of trainees, takes us into a classroom to demonstrate how to use the banks of ten switches by every classroom door, which variously control the lights and blinds. I try to dim the lights but open the blinds instead.

Later, when I try to engage my fellow maths teachers in general chat, I notice a certain reticence. They haven't seen each other all summer, but after the briefest of hugs and exchanges about their holidays they are head down, looking at their new class lists. This is also a big departure from my old life. Teachers are busy. They don't chat.

Before lunch we file into a classroom and are given a quiz about the school. Why did the school's founder decide to name the school after himself? I put up my hand.

'Ego?'

The teacher leading the session looks embarrassed. 'Interesting!' she says. 'I hadn't thought of that!'

A more experienced teacher volunteers the correct answer: 'Strong family values.' I resolve to abandon all cynicism, which has served me so well in my career so far.

Over lunch I meet my mentor, who will be responsible for me and my progress. Liam has already told me that he has had to give careful thought to finding the right person to look after me – a great deal of experience will be required. I try to unpack this. Does he think I will be slow to learn, or that I'll be obstreperous? I don't think I will be either. (As it turns out, I'll be both.)

Yasmeen is a 35-year-old matriarch of Pakistani extraction with a face set to 'severe' but which intermittently breaks into a radiant smile. I look at her long nails painted shiny maroon, and fold my own wrinkled hands into a fist. I don't want her to see the dirt that has collected under my broken nails after a summer of gardening.

She tells me how she came to England from Lahore as a teenage bride, worked as a receptionist to make money while at the same time studying for an Open University degree in maths. Six weeks after the birth of her second child, she trained with Teach First and six years later she is number two in the maths department. I listen to her story and feel sheepish: the courage of her entry to the profession makes mine look puny.

Yasmeen: I googled you and saw a travel article you wrote about flying around the world in a private plane! Why are you giving that up?!

Me: I've had enough. I want to do what you do.

Yasmeen (*looking sceptical*): If you get any more free holidays, can I come too?

That night I say to my recorder: 'I love Yasmeen. She's tough and scary, but she's also warm and a laugh. I think we're going to get on brilliantly.'

On the dot of 8.13am the following morning nearly 200 11-year-olds in oversized brand-new grey-and-red blazers are shown how to line up with perfect military precision. The entire teaching staff prowl up and down reprimanding children whose ties are not tied tightly enough or whose backpacks are not neatly placed on the ground by their right heel. One boy is so scared he leaves the line to throw up by the basketball hoops. The teachers assure me this happens every year, and don't seem too troubled by it. I'm feeling a bit like throwing up myself.

I also feel torn. The school is built on the broken windows theory of policing – pupils who get yelled at for putting their hands in their pockets are less likely to throw desks or stab each other. They are more likely to do the homework, get decent results and have a better start in life. I get that and I strongly approve. But then I look at the vomiting child: is this the best way to deal with children who are nervous about their first day of school?

The following day the rest of the school arrives. Now there are 1,500 pupils lined up in the playground, motionless, silent and staring straight in front of them.

I thought I'd be profoundly grateful to be protected by such a rigid regime. Students at this school do not dare say 'boo' to a goose – which is mighty reassuring if you happen to be as big a goose as I am. But at the same time the fear being instilled in the teenagers is rubbing off on me – my stomach is churning and there's a metallic taste in my mouth. I left journalism because I wanted to be afraid. It seems to me now that I should have been more careful what I wished for.

For the first two weeks I'm meant to be spending time observing my colleagues teach, taking notes so that I can copy them myself. I watch Yasmeen's preternatural calm as she faces a class of teenagers. How can I replicate that when my anxiety level is so high the students can almost certainly smell it?

Yasmeen tells me that from next week I'm going to take over her top set Year 8 class. 'These kids are very smart,' she says. 'Do not tell them you're a trainee. The most important thing is that they respect you as a mathematician.'

This, I think, is going to be a challenge given my dwindling respect for myself in that area. My decision to teach maths, taken so lightly a year earlier, now seems flimsy. I last did any maths in 1977 and only got a B at A level and now every morning I try to do half an hour of mental maths to limber up. This morning my brain balked at 17 x 31.

Yasmeen tells me to print out the class photographs for 8R1. Where do I find them, I ask? How do I use the printer? She sighs and does it herself. She hands me a printout of 32 passport-sized pictures with names underneath, and tells me to get to work on a seating plan. She has warned me that Henry and Hassain are naughty and Khadija and Imran are lazy. They should all be where I can see them. I cut the photos out, rearranging them and memorising their unfamiliar names.

Then she tells me to look at the scheme of work to see what I should be teaching them. What is the scheme of work, I ask? Where is it? I know I'm annoying her, but I'm not sure what else to do. She fishes a spreadsheet out of a file on her computer, glances at it and says my first lesson is on index laws.

What's that, I ask? Fixing me with her most disapproving stare, she explains. 'Ah!' I say. 'It's what we used to call "powers" in the 1970s.' Yasmeen does not look terribly reassured.

I set about preparing for my first class – I have read that you should never spend longer planning a lesson than giving it. The lesson lasts 55 minutes; my planning takes four days. The first challenge is a piece of software called SMART Notebook. Throughout my career I have despised PowerPoint from afar – writing scornful columns about it, but never deigning to use it. SMART Notebook turns out to be PowerPoint on steroids and is sheerest hell if you are dumb with computers.

Index numbers are a particular curse. It takes six different keystrokes to add one to a slide, after which the tiny number has to be dragged into place. On my slides, none of them are quite lined up, giving my examples a drunken, raffish air. Yasmeen looks at my lesson plan and frowns. That bit is too complicated, she says. That bit is too easy. That bit should come after that bit. I start all over again.

On the day of the lesson I wake up at 4am, wired and fearful. Two hours later I am at school, standing in an empty classroom. With some difficulty I get my slides onto the SMART Board and practise writing on the whiteboard next to it with my arm at an awkward angle so that I can see the empty desks while I write. Never turn your back on the classroom, Yasmeen has warned me.

At the beginning of period 3 Yasmeen goes down to collect the class from line-up. I watch through the window as they march across the playground, my heart hammering in my throat. Thirty-two of the school's brightest 12-year-olds advance along the corridor, silent and in single file. I have been told how to stand by the door as they come in. 'Good morning!' I say.

'Good morning, Miss,' they reply.

I feel a jolt of pleasure. They called me Miss! They don't seem surprised by me! I'm just another teacher! They file in, look at the seating plan on the board and sit down in their places. Yasmeen sits at the back, notebook open on her lap.

I start the reflection that begins every lesson at the school: 'Throughout this class,' I begin. A stir goes round the room.

'Throughout this *lesson*,' one of the students corrects me.

'Oops,' I say. More giggling. This is not a great start.

The starter exercise goes without a hitch. The students work silently for five minutes after which I put up a slide with the answers on it.

'Miss, can you make that bigger, please?' says a bespectacled boy in the front row.

I go to the computer but can't get the mouse off the whiteboard. 'Go to "zoom",' someone in the class calls out. By now I have lost control of the mouse – and the class, which is gawping and giggling.

I glance at Yasmeen who is giving me her sternest 'what the hell??' expression. She gets up and comes to the front where she fixes the problem in two seconds. I offer up thanks for the strictness of this school. In a more freewheeling place the kids would be throwing tables by now.

Order restored, I start to go through my careful examples, after which the students try on their own. I think it's going fine, but Yasmeen is scowling and gesturing at me from the back of the room. Flustered, I try to clarify something on the white-board but get so mixed up I multiply rather than add the powers. A kid points out my mistake, and I say 'Oops' again, which makes them smirk again. I wander around the class looking at their work: they mostly seem to be getting it all right. I assume this means I'm a good teacher after all. It hasn't occurred to me they can do this because they are bright and they did it last year.

Almost no sooner than it began, the lesson is over. This is the most remarkable thing about teaching – how fast the time goes.

'How do you feel?' asks Yasmeen, leading me back to our office to give feedback.

'Relieved,' I say.

I am also wet with sweat. There are great circles under my arms and my hair is stuck to my head. I remember some advice given by a teacher on how to survive the first term, which at the time I thought was an exaggeration. 'Wear a jacket you hate – you'll sweat so much it'll never recover.'

On a sheet of A4 paper, Yasmeen has drawn two columns headed WWW and EBI – 'What Went Well' and 'Even Better If'. In my previous life I would have scorned these euphemistic acronyms – now I must take them seriously.

What went well, it turns out, is I have a good teacher pres-ence. Also, the starter activity was well chosen – though the triumph of this is lessened by the fact that Yasmeen suggested it herself.

What went badly was everything else. The EBI column contains 23 items, starting:

Too fast
Mistake on board
You said 'Shhh'
You let Henry call out
Workings not clear
Jamal didn't understand
Yunus was looking out of the window

Yasmeen assures me there are too many things to fix by next lesson, so she will give me only one: sort out the technology.

Tomorrow I have the same class for a double lesson – almost two hours of teaching – and I haven't started planning. I stay up until 1am preparing my slides and rehearse my explanations to myself in the mirror, and the next day, stressed and bleary, I make more mistakes on the board. I make a hash of explaining negative powers, and spend too long on the first example. Worse still, I get so muddled I write on the SMART Board with the whiteboard pen. I try to rub the mark off with my hand, but at my touch the slide moves on to the next one, and I have no idea how to get it back.

But when it is over and Yasmeen has gone through an interminable new list of EBIs, I feel bizarrely buoyant. I know there is a lot that is wrong, but I know the biggest thing is right. I went into this with one fixed idea – that I would love standing in front of a class. I have now proved that, mostly, I do. Smaller things are right too: I already know the pupils' names. They seem to want to learn. I definitely want to teach them.

In psychology, there is a famous curve that plots confidence against knowledge. When you start something confidence runs high. At the beginning you have the courage of the stupid: you do not know enough to realise just how bad you are. This is exactly where I am now.

On Friday I go for drinks with my maths colleagues. There are 15 of us in the department, of whom a hard core of eight are regular pub-goers. We start drinking at 4.45pm and an hour later I've already had three bottles of lager and am thoroughly enjoying myself. They seem interested in what I used to do and are mystified as to why I would have taken a pay cut to be a teacher. But they can see how keen I am and I think they are flattered that I have chosen to do what they do. As I get up to buy another round, my new friends express their appreciation. 'Lucy! Lucy!' they chant, banging their empty glasses on the pub tables.

I return with drinks, glowing inside at how well I'm fitting in. But then Roisin, a 25-year-old teacher from Ireland who I've already singled out as a future friend, turns to me and says: 'You really remind me of my grandmother.'

*

Two weeks later I take over another class. This is a bottom set Year 7, and the regular teacher for this class is Anne. She is a mere decade younger than me, has been a teacher all her life, and from the beginning I sense trouble. Anne also does not understand why I'm doing this and thinks it's all a publicity stunt. 'I've read your article,' she says darkly, offering no further comment.

My first lesson is ordering fractions. I have planned something explaining why ½ is smaller than ¾, but as I go through the proof, the class of 11-year-olds fidgets and squirms. They don't have a clue what I'm talking about.

I make it easier. Which is bigger: ½ or ¼? A forest of hands goes up. They all say ¼. I draw some pizzas on the board to disabuse them of this. They get it, I think.

Afterwards Anne says that for this class all that matters is behaviour – and that behaviour in my lesson was terrible. I must never start talking if any child is fiddling with a ruler. I must give detentions to anyone who is not giving their full attention, and if they do something truly shocking, like turning round, send them out of the room.

At the time I'm outraged, as I thought the behaviour was fine.

'Can you believe it?' I whisper mutinously to another trainee as we eat our school dinners. 'Another example of extremism by this ridiculous school.'

Fiddling with a ruler, we agree, is not bad behaviour – in any case, surely a dedicated fiddler can grasp negative numbers better if their fingers are bending and unbending their hinged ruler. But now, several years into teaching, I'm much less sure. When you are explaining something you need every student in the class to listen. The fiddling might do no harm to the fiddler, but it's distracting for fellow classmates and for the teacher. I've turned hardcore: all fiddling needs stamping out.

Next lesson, during which it emerges that most of the class remains devoted to the view that ¼ is bigger than ½, I give lunchtime detentions to 14 out of a total of 20 for variously fiddling with pens or talking or sitting slouched in their chairs. They duly turn up, along with a sweet but chaotic Year 8 boy to whom I've also given a detention for not doing his homework in the right colour pen.

There ensues 20 minutes of noisy chaos, after which the Year 8 boy stays behind to tell me that he has never seen anything so out-of-control at this school.

'I feel sorry for you, Miss,' he says.

To be pitied by a 12-year-old feels very bitter indeed.

The next day I walk into school with a heavy heart. The unfamiliar and unwanted thought that I really might not be any good at this is starting to occur to me. I have lived my whole life avoiding things I'm bad at. I play no ball games. I avoid saying anything in a foreign language. I don't play Scrabble. I don't sing in public. Or dance. As I've got older I have concentrated on the things I do well, as a result of which I've got better at them.

The experience of being bad at something is both unfamiliar and hard to deal with, though not in the way you might expect. I don't mind telling Radio 4 listeners that I'm bad, because that makes good copy. I don't even mind telling myself. This would have been crucifying if I were 22 but, as it is, I have the perfect ego-saving excuse. Being bad at teaching does not make me a worthless person, because I've proved I'm good at other things. This thought is allowing my ego to hold up, just about.

By contrast, what I am finding borderline unmanageable is being seen as hopeless by my colleagues and, even worse, by my students. This is mortifying and makes me feel I'm letting the side down. None of them could care less that I used to write decent columns on the *FT*. The students have never heard of it, and if some of the teachers have, it makes no difference. All that matters is here and now. And in the here and now, I'm failing.

'How long are you going to stick with teaching?' Anne asks during one particularly bad post-mortem.

Out of nowhere comes my defiant answer: I am going to teach until I'm 75. She looks incredulous, but the more incredulous she is, the more determined I am to prove her wrong. I have thrown down the gauntlet to myself – if I managed a total of 35 years as a journalist, surely I can do 17 as a teacher?

As for what I must do now, I must improve. My daughter Rose, who is now training teachers in Ghana, rings me every night on WhatsApp for a pep talk. 'Mum, it sounds like you're being amazing! Everyone finds it hard at first!' she says, night after night.

Good trainees are meant to reflect constantly on their progress. I remind myself I am getting better at some things. I can just about manage the computer system. I can keep my explanations tighter. But there is a huge thing that is holding me back. Carelessness has dogged me all my life, but now I must change, or else I won't survive. I make too many mathematical mistakes and there are too many typos on my slides – I have to find a way of transitioning from a careless person to a slightly more accurate one.

About six weeks into my new life I get an email from an old contact I had when I was a journalist.

Hi Lucy!
Hope you're well. Are you enjoying teaching?? Which day is best for you to catch up over coffee or lunch?

I look at this and feel the size of the gap between my current world and my old one. The answer to the second question is easy. No day is good for a coffee or lunch. Teachers work all day, five days a week, so lunch and coffees no longer exist. The weekend's no good either. I'm simply too tired.

The answer to the first is even easier. No, I'm not enjoying teaching. It is not enjoyable to be out of control – to find you've come to the classroom without exercise books so the whole class has to do their work on pieces of paper – and then your head of department comes in to ask what you're doing.

'Enjoy' is altogether the wrong word. A better word might be 'obsessed'. Never have I been this engaged with anything in my professional life. I think about nothing else from the moment I wake up pre-dawn. My students visit me in my sleep and are with me as I get up, wired, at 5.30. My head is filled with the same ragged euphoric sensation I last had when I was in love.

This obsession is making me tiresome to my friends. I have only one topic of conversation, which means I can only see people who can tolerate it. All of my children are strongly behind me, though only my eldest has the patience to hear me out. The old colleagues who thought this a crazy move I am avoiding. I need to prove them wrong before I can safely meet them.

At half-term, after the most intense eight weeks of my working life, I go to Cornwall with my friend Emma, whom I've known since university and who has worked at the *Economist* for as long as I worked at the *FT*. As she talks about her work, I listen almost with pity – why on earth is she still, decades in, writing and editing articles at the same place? It seems so evident to me that the excitement is all mine, and the drudgery all hers.

I've taken some exam papers to mark, and as I sit by the fire correcting students' work I challenge her to the Year 8 maths paper. She, who has an Oxford PPE degree and is one of the cleverest people I know, scores a feeble 59 per cent. Gleefully, I assure her she would be at the bottom of my class. After a couple of days she goes home. I think she is relieved to leave – and I think I'm relieved to be on my own. I'm not really fit for company at all.

When I go back after half-term I seem to have got worse at teaching – which might be because I'm actually going backwards, or because I'm sliding down the confidence curve. Either way, Anne tells me that she's 'surprised' at how sloppy my marking is. Yasmeen tells me that my modelling on the board is a mess. Anne tells me my handouts are too scruffy and I must guillotine them so they fit neatly into exercise books. Yasmeen tells me I hand out sheets inefficiently.

I tell myself I'm on the verge of not coping. I'm only teaching eight hours a week – compared to 22 hours for a qualified teacher – but am overwhelmed by how much planning this requires.

The head of maths comes to observe me. She herself is a phenomenally good teacher: exacting, hard-working and relentlessly keen on detail. I am eager to impress and have planned a careful lesson teaching Year 7s to solve worded problems. I have composed a worksheet using their names – 'Paris goes on a picnic with one cake to share between her friends, Rasan and Hamid' – and fancy this makes them settle down to do the task with rather more enthusiasm than usual.

The department head invites me into her office afterwards to deliver her feedback. She begins with the inevitable: 'How did you think that went?'

'Good!' I say.

She frowns and tells me the things I know I'm bad at: careless modelling, not enough structure, too many students calling out answers. But then she says the reason they were calling out was that they were excited and – here was the heart of the problem – I had made them excited by being excited myself.

I look at her goody-goody plait and seethe. I want to say: I fundamentally disagree with your view on education. These are very low-ability kids. Anything that makes them excited is good. And I would much rather have an exciting teacher than a boring one. More than that, I want to say: Shove your job. I refuse to be a robot.

For a minute I long for the *FT*. If a subeditor wanted to question even a word in one of my columns, they would send me a polite email asking permission. I was in charge, to be deferred to as a matter of course. That was another world. For now, I have to get a grip. Be humble, I tell myself. Be grateful. Be professional.

'Thank you so much,' I say. 'That is really useful feedback.' I repeat her messages back to her, and say I will strive to put them right at once. I might not be good at teaching but I am good at office politics, having built up my skill over 30 years. This time, I am pretty sure I nailed it: I don't think she can see the mutiny behind my eyes.

I buckle down and try to do better. I cut my handouts to size and try not to sound excited. But I am constantly disappointed at how slow my progress is, even though I increasingly recognise this as both arrogant and unrealistic. It took me at least ten years to be any good as a journalist, so why would I expect to crack teaching (which I'm finding much harder) in ten weeks?

Not all the feedback is dismal. Nhung, a bright, hardworking girl in my Year 8 class, lacks confidence and I have spent some time after lessons helping her. She hands me a Christmas card containing a long letter of gratitude in her neatest writing, ending: 'You are the best maths teacher EVER.'

This is evidently not true, but I take it. The next weekend I bump into Nhung outside the Vietnamese nail parlour by my house. 'Miss Kellaway!' she beams. She says her aunt works inside and I go inside and for the first time in my life get my nails done. I tell Nhung's aunt that she should be proud of her niece. She looks briefly confounded but then smiles.

After February half-term I spend six weeks teaching at another Hackney comprehensive – you can't become a trained teacher unless you have experience of two different schools.

On my first day I'm standing outside the gates ogling the stubby tie of one of the pupils and longing to tell him to re-tie it properly. This school, though relatively well behaved by national standards, has none of the military precision that I'm now used to. The kids are milling around and there is a roar of noise.

I'm going to get eaten alive, I think. My new mentor, Mike, energetic ex-Teach Firster who is less than half my age and is standing by my side, is thinking exactly the same thing.

I know this because on my last day he tells me so.

Mike: When they told me I was going to be mentoring someone who was 58, I thought: This isn't going to work.
Me: That wasn't very open-minded of you.
Mike: And then I googled you, and I thought: Oh, God. This is going to be a car crash.
Me: And it was, wasn't it?
Mike: When I saw you in that first lesson, and you were flapping around and couldn't change the slides, I just thought: Jesus.

Right now he is doing a good job of not letting his fears show as he lets me loose on his top set Year 9 class. It doesn't go well. I can't make my presentation work and so am trying to explain the substitution method for simultaneous equations on the whiteboard, when one girl pipes up: 'I'm not being funny, Miss. But I could learn this better from watching a video.'

Afterwards Mike tells me it wasn't too bad (which it was). He advises that every time a child misbehaves I give them a behaviour point and write their name on the board. I try this in the next lesson.

> Me: Roman, that's a behaviour point. (*writes name on board*)
> Student: My name isn't Roman.
> Me (*confounded*): What *is* your name?
> Student: It's Isaac, Miss. (*laughter*)
> Me: OK, Isaac, you have a behaviour point.
> Student 2: *I'm* Isaac. (*whole class starts hooting*)

At the end of the lesson there is a long list of names on the board, which I plan to enter into the detention system at break. Only I never get to do this as, behind my back, one of the students has wiped the whole list off the board as they left the classroom.

In one of my new classes I teach an autistic boy who puts his hands over his ears and drums his feet in distress every time the class gets disorderly – which is several times a lesson. At the end of one class he starts to cry and I sit with him, unsure of how to console him. Through his sobs he chokes: 'Everyone hates you, Miss. We want Mr McAulay back.'

I was so intent on comforting him that the weight of the blow took a while to land. I tramped home that night through the snow that had made London white and still in March and called Rose in Ghana. 'Don't worry, Mum,' she said. 'Students always say they hate you one minute and love you the next. You must ignore all of it.'

I fought on, and Mike took me in hand. After a few weeks my classes were becoming marginally less unruly and sometimes I felt that the students had actually learnt something. On my last day the radio producer came in to record my final session with my most difficult class. At the end of the lesson I told them they would not see me again as I was returning to my other school – whereupon, with one breath the whole class whooped: 'Yesss!' My shame was balanced by a more familiar feeling from my old life: This will make great radio.

My students might not have been sad to see the back of me, but I was sad to go. I liked the camaraderie of the staffroom and loved our Friday nights at the pub, where in sheer relief that the week had come to an end I'd started drinking shots, and even in extremis would go up to the pub's cold roof with Mike to smoke the odd cigarette – a habit I'd chucked 30 years earlier. I even wondered if he'd make a good match for one of my daughters.

After I'd left, Mike emailed me to say that my most dreaded pupil, the one who'd declared I was worse than a video, said to him when he took the class back: 'Miss Kellaway – yeah, she wasn't too bad in the end.' This was the most encouraging feedback I'd received since I started teaching.

Back at my regular school for the last term I was given two new classes, a middle set Year 9 and a bottom set Year 10.

Even though I was still pretty incompetent, I was getting used to feeling mildly out of control and was less discombobulated by it. I was sleeping later and relaxing more. Not everything was improving, however.

On one boiling day in the summer term I was teaching trigonometry to Year 9. I was in mid-flow; and saw a member of the school's senior leadership team was standing in the doorway glowering.

Senior leader: Can I have a word?

Me: Yes?

Senior leader: Your sandals are backless! (*points at Birkenstocks*) You aren't allowed to teach in those! Have you got any other shoes in school? Otherwise you must go home and change.

Me: What, now? But I'm halfway through the lesson.

Senior leader: Yes, now.

I left the room in disgrace followed by 32 pairs of eyes. By some fluke I had another pair of shoes downstairs, so I put them on and returned to the class, which had fallen silent now that I was no longer in it. The senior leader checked my shoes and left the classroom without a word.

In order to qualify as a teacher every trainee in the country has to provide a fat folder of evidence that they have met the government's eight teaching standards – including planning, behaviour management and setting high expectations. This part of my course was run by King's College London, and sometimes on Saturdays, exhausted, I went for training days there with one of the other Now Teachers from my school. Assembling the evidence was a gargantuan job which I did perfunctorily, as the qualification is pass/fail and I couldn't see how filling in a folder was going to help me be a better teacher. I don't know how minutely anyone at King's studied the scrappy documents I eventually handed in, but it seemed to pass whatever mysterious minimum standard had been set.

When one day in June 2018 I finally qualified, it was all a bit of an anticlimax. The email went into my spam folder, and I found it only by accident a few days later when I was looking for something else. I had Qualified Teacher Status.

I didn't feel especially proud, even though I had learnt more in ten months than in any period of my life. I had got a bit better with technology, I mainly came to lessons with the right things, and though I was still careless, I was trying hard. I'd learnt how to look frightening, and how to enter detentions correctly in the system. I could, more or less, teach.

But at some point in the year I'd realised that something was fundamentally wrong. The problem wasn't just that I was inexperienced, but that I was never going to be as good at teaching maths as some of the younger teachers, who were both more orderly and better at the subject. Maybe the head of maths was right. I was too excited. I wanted my students to be excited. I wanted to be able to have animated discussions with them.

I decided I needed a change of subject. One of the many oddities about teacher training is that once you qualify you can teach anything at all – which meant I didn't have to plough on with maths but could teach economics, which I not only had a degree in, but had spent nearly four decades thinking about.

As luck would have it, another school in the same academy chain in Hackney was looking for an economics and business studies teacher. I applied and was duly interviewed, which meant giving a lesson to a class of teenagers I'd never met, on a subject I'd never taught, watched by the head teacher.

Instead of being terrified, I felt good as I embarked on my lesson on the adverse effects of unemployment because, for once, I knew what I was talking about. Afterwards, the head talked to me as if I was a grown-up rather than the wayward child I'd been as a trainee, and I even dared ask if I could do the job three days a week, which would mean that I could spend the rest of the time working on promoting Now Teach. He said I could.

My first day as a Newly Qualified Teacher in September 2018 bore no relation to my first day a year earlier. I was still afraid, but manageably so. Teaching is a hierarchy and as a Newly Qualified Teacher, I'd advanced one critical rung up the ladder. I had my own classes to teach for ever. I was trusted with a set of keys to the classroom. I wasn't observed all the time. I could even do playground duty alone.

The biggest change was my new boss, Marcel. Marcel was almost my age, had worked at other things before, and was a warm hulk of a man, much loved by students.

'You're going to be great,' he said to me, before he'd even seen me teach. 'You've got so much life experience. The students will love that.' Marcel was sure I could do it, which made me think maybe I could, after all.

In my first lesson teaching business studies I screwed up. Afterwards I went straight to Marcel, fearing another Birkenstock incident.

Me: What colour are the business studies exercise books?

Marcel: Yellow.

Me: Oh, God! I gave them purple ones! I'm so sorry! What shall I do?

Marcel: No biggie.

From that moment I loved him. Marcel was going to protect me from the system, support me and keep me sane. He also made me laugh, on one memorable occasion, dancing around the tiny office we shared with maths teachers singing: 'I'm too sexy for my shirt.'

It's the annual staff Christmas party in my second year teaching economics. We are in a room at the local pub and I'm having a shouted conversation over the noise to a colleague who is in charge of all NQTs and who has watched me teach many times.

> Isobel: Do you miss your old life?
> Me: No. Never.
> Isobel: That's great to hear! So you're enjoying teaching?
> Me: Yes – finally. It's taken a while, but I really am.
> Isobel: I'm not surprised. If you were a stick of rock, you'd have 'teacher' written all the way through you.

My mum, who most definitely had 'teacher' written all through her too, would have winced at my repeating this. She taught me never to accept compliments on the grounds that they were rarely sincere, and on no account ever to repeat them to third parties. She also taught me to hate a tired metaphor.

But I don't care. I am going to accept this one. Whether it is true or not, no other compliment in my life has made me quite so happy.

6

Old Dogs, New Tricks

The first Now Teach trainee to throw in the towel was the last person I would have expected. Matthew was a 60-year-old ex-banker, who had previously convinced himself (and me) that his true calling in life was to transmit his love of Shakespeare to the disadvantaged youth of West London. Alas, after barely a month of teaching, his doctor had signed him off for stress, and a couple of weeks after that he rang me to say he was leaving. He had looked around at the harassed teachers in his staffroom and decided their way of working was not sustainable. I was all set to guilt-trip him into staying, but then thought if the job was making him ill, perhaps I should lay off. With heavy heart I said I understood – which of course I didn't.

The next week Alan, an engineer who had spent a successful career at a big construction company, walked into the principal's office at the school in South London where he was teaching science and quit. He later told me he was too lonely in the classroom. He'd spent his life working in teams with other grown-ups and felt isolated with only teenagers to talk to. Again, I let him go nicely, but inside I was raging. What the bloody hell did he expect? Didn't he notice that the thing about schools is that they have children in them?

Alec was the next to fall. He had been one of my favourites, a gentle aspiring chemistry teacher who had spent a career in the City. He had a problem in his family that meant flying off to Canada to sort it out. This wasn't his fault – and this time I did understand.

Then came Sebastian, who used to be a management consultant but had opted to teach geography. I'd heard he was wobbling and went to remonstrate with him in his charming house in Notting Hill, where he told me point blank that he was done – teaching struck him as simply too little fun and too much work for too little money. There was nothing to say to this, but to shrug, fume inwardly, and let him go.

The final straw was Edward, who over the past few months had become a good friend. Edward had worked in the media all his life, was sophisticated, hilarious, and so cynical he made me seem like Pollyanna. He had become fed up with how dumbed down telly had become, and had decided he wanted to be an English teacher instead. Now he was struggling. Like me he was catastrophically poor with technology and his natural tendency to doubt everything meant he was finding the culture at his academy school hard to swallow. He, too, was done.

I phoned Katie in a panic. We were barely two months in and already we were five down. This was going to be a catastrophe. It seemed I was the Pied Piper, after all – the rats had followed me to the banks of the river and now they were all going to drown.

Only they didn't. Just before Christmas the rats who were still swimming gathered in ARK's Reception area for cold takeaway pizza and warm Prosecco. I looked around the room and noted that almost everyone looked half a stone lighter, that most reported never having been so tired, but not one of them was talking of quitting. Instead everyone seemed to have got bizarrely younger, sharpened and lightened by their raw energy. They felt about this roughly as I did: it was brutal and brilliant, in equal measure. Before teaching we had all been, one way or another, a bit stuck, but now we were all high on adrenaline and, in a masochistic kind of way, were loving it.

In the end, the final tally of quitters was 12 out of 45. Though I'd lost my bet, I comforted myself by moving the goal posts. I now see that my original estimate of two was madly unrealistic, as was my authoritarian (and futile) ban on quitting. Teacher training is hard and no one of any age can really know if they are going to like it until they try it. What was remarkable about our first year was not that so many dropped out, but that so few did. You might have expected the failure rate among Now Teachers to be higher than among trainees 30 years younger, but in fact it was slightly lower.

Each year since that hair-raising first one, we have hired more people and a higher percentage of them have survived. There were 75 who started the following year, 85 the next one and 140 the year after that, of whom more than four-fifths have stuck with it.

Now Teach is no longer me, Katie and Rebecca crouching in a canteen, trying to figure out how a spreadsheet works. We have a recruitment team, a marketing team and three further people who look after the trainees in schools, hold their hands through the inevitable crises, and organise events. We have money from the government and seem to have somehow become an efficient and professional machine.

Four years in, I no longer feel even slightly guilty to the Pied Piper charge. At our regular information evenings I tell everyone straight – this is hard. It is then up to them to decide whether they fancy it – and up to us to weed out the ones who we think are not going to make it. This is also hard. From the outset I have not only been useless at predicting the overall number of drop-outs but at guessing which ones will quit. Most of the people I was worried about at interview have turned into excellent teachers, while a few of the ones I thought would fly have crashed on impact.

Some people drop out because life has intervened – a dying parent suddenly needs caring for – which is random, though more likely to happen to a 50-year-old trainee than to a 25-year-old one. The rest quit for reasons that are also hard to spot in advance – they simply find they don't like teaching as much as they thought they would.

Yet there are a few things we have learnt to look out for that lengthen the chances of someone sticking with it. The first is a mixture of selfishness and altruism. The best Now Teachers need to want the challenge because they think it will make them feel better or be happier – they want it for themselves. They also need to want to help children learn – which is more selfless.

If candidates have only the first motive, they are unlikely to get through the selection process. I remember talking to one alpha-male former bond dealer who wanted to be a maths teacher. He went on and on about the great kick he got from getting out of his comfort zone, and how this would be the toughest challenge he had yet met. 'Failure is not an option for me,' he said.

In the course of this chest thumping, he didn't mention education or children once – or anything apart from himself. We didn't give him the chance to fail. He was missing the altruistic urge, which is central to survival – if you don't really care about whether your students learn, it's probably not going to work.

Caring about students in the abstract isn't enough to survive as a teacher. You need to enjoy spending time with them. This was Alan's undoing – he simply found he didn't enjoy their company enough. It also helps if you like your subject. I nearly came unstuck in my first year when I found out on closer acquaintance that I didn't want to spend my life with right-angled triangles, teaching kids to memorise SOHCAHTOA. Now I'm teaching economics I get so excited at the thought of a ballooning budget deficit that I often catch my students exchanging amused glances.

Finally, teachers need to be resilient. This, I'd thought, was a given for my generation, as it's hard to have survived 30 years at work without having picked up some toughness on the way. One way and another, I was sure we'd all be fine. Here, again, I was wrong.

Week three, I was sitting at my shared computer in the dark maths office at school when I got a text from Clive, a 55-year-old former banker with a first in French from Cambridge and a booming voice, who was now training to be a language teacher in my school.

His message said:

I HATE THIS. I WANT TO LEAVE. NOW.

What a baby, I thought to myself. I sighed and went over to the languages block to find him. We hid in an empty classroom and I spent an hour trying to talk him down from the ledge. I told him my first lessons had been appalling too, but I knew I would get better – as would he. I told him how valuable he would be as a first-rate linguist to the Alevel students, and how he could help prepare them for the finest universities. I don't think any of it went in. His 22-year-old son, with whom he had dinner that evening, was less delicate – but more effective. He told his father to man up. And so, at least for a bit, Clive swallowed his pride, dealt with the fact that he was no longer a master of the universe but a teacher who had so far failed to earn the respect of a class of 12-year-olds, and set about the long business of winning them round. Though he became a good teacher, he didn't quite finish the year, dropping out at the last moment (however, he has now returned to teaching students in an A-level college, which seems to suit everyone).

If the sample of that year was anything to go by, the women turned out to be on average tougher than the men. I have a theory this may be because early failures in the classroom are humiliating for everyone, but women may be better at dealing with it. They don't see it as a blow to their very being, but are more likely to be pragmatic, get on with it and let it pass. Sophie, a former journalist, decided that the best way of dealing with her own Sisyphean struggles in her school was to broadcast them to the rest of us on our group WhatsApp.

I've been placed on an Enhanced Support Plan by my mentor. I told her my best quality was resilience – and my motto was 'Fall down 8 times, stand up 7' – or … er … is it the other way round??

'Enhanced Criticism Plan, more like,' a fellow Now Teacher texted in support. 'Keep at it, Soph.' And she did.

So long as the motivation was right and the loins sufficiently girded, I thought we'd learn quickly. We'd pick up the skills faster because we were older and wiser. In fact, I was slower to learn than most young teachers, and so were many of the others. And some of us, with me a shining example, were dunces with technology – at first I couldn't even take the register because I couldn't open the right piece of dratted software without losing the slides on the screen.

Yet for most of us learning proved less of a problem than unlearning. It's not exactly that you can't teach an old dog new tricks. You absolutely can. What is hard is getting the dog to unlearn its old ones. It was this unlearning of decades of experience of working at other things that proved hard for almost all of us, and was the undoing of a few.

Simon was one of the most promising candidates I'd ever seen. An ex-investment banker whose own life had been changed by teachers, who really wanted to do good, and who also was a serious mathematician – he was my pin-up Now Teacher. I was so certain that Simon would be great I nabbed him for my own school, where they were so impressed by him at interview they asked if I had any more like him up my sleeve. For a term he sat next to me in the maths office so that I could look after him – but instead of flourishing as I'd been sure he would, he seemed increasingly stressed, and by Christmas he'd left.

What went wrong with Simon was he found it hard to unlearn the ways of working he'd picked up in big corporations. The chaos of school is surprising and unsettling and he struggled to understand that things did not proceed according to a spreadsheet and that, instead, he was meant to roll up his sleeves and get on with it.

At least Simon was a modest sort of man and didn't have to unlearn the most difficult thing of all: self-importance. In our old lives, most of us were people with opinions that were sought out by others, while in our new life we had to get used to the idea that, as know-nothing trainees, our views didn't count. In his previous life, Robert was a senior partner at a City law firm, and was used to having captains of industry pay through the nose for his advice. Within his first weeks at school he was telling his colleagues what he thought of the way the school was run (not much). One of them tipped him off that this wasn't going down well coming from a trainee – and he took note. He unlearnt the expectation that everyone needed to hear his views and kept his mouth shut until he'd earned the right to express them. Things went better after that.

Once we all figured out how to do things and how to comport ourselves – which for most of us took the best part of a year – I fancy that an odd switch has happened. Instead of struggling more with our work than our younger colleagues, Now Teachers are struggling less. Now, four years

117

in, I don't think teaching is unsustainable. I think it's the reverse.

One of my best friends at school is 27. Serena and I have a great deal in common – we are both natural show-offs who talk a lot. We spend our days doing exactly the same thing under the same regime. We stand at the front of a class and try to interest the kids in parallel lines or price equilibrium. We have the same struggles when lessons go badly, and the same joys when previously lazy kids suddenly pull their fingers out. We are both teachers because we like being with teenagers and think this is a useful thing for us to be doing with our time.

For all the similarities, the difference between us is 34 years, which means Serena's motivation is different. She has just bought a minuscule flat and needs more money to help her pay the mortgage. She is ambitious and wants to feel she is progressing. Her self-esteem is invested in being good at this job, as is her bank balance. Even after a big promotion she carries a weight of stress and anxiety that I am entirely without.

My position, and that of about two-thirds of the Now Teachers, is quite different. We have no desire to advance above the bottom rung of the ladder that we are now squarely standing on. We own our own property and don't need to prove ourselves in the same way she does. We don't want to be promoted, but only want to be responsible for our own classes and for becoming better at what we do. That feels quite enough.

This resistance to promotion makes us both happier and harder to manage. In my second year teaching economics I get called into my boss's office.

Chris: Thanks for popping in, Luce. I won't beat about the bush: would you like to be economics subject lead?
Me: Will it involve filling in spreadsheets or managing anyone else?
Chris: Well, yes, but it's a promotion! You'd get more money.
Me: No thanks. I only want to teach my students.
Chris (*pleading*): It'd look good on your CV ...
Me: My CV can take care of itself.

Because of this aversion to promotion, I have a different sort of relationship with my manager. I hope he likes me and can see I'm trying hard to be a good teacher. But if not, then so be it. I don't need to impress him because my future does not depend on his approval. This removes a great deal of anxiety – while my young colleagues worry endlessly about whether they are in trouble, I seldom give it a second thought.

There is another big difference between me and Serena. I work three days a week and she works five. About 60 per cent of Now Teachers teach part-time, which is an option not open to most of the younger teachers, as they can't afford it. Working three days a week means we are not tired or overwhelmed, it means we have more time to spend marking and preparing, and allows us actively to enjoy what we do. One year, when I was timetabled with both Thursdays and Fridays off, I found my heart lifted on Mondays upon seeing my students again. At the end of term when my colleagues are on their knees, I'm fairly perky. Sometimes I have to pretend to be exhausted so as not to be too annoying.

There is another, odder benefit we have over our young colleagues, which I never expected, and which I stumbled on by accident.

When I decided to be a teacher, I thought I'd gone post-status. It no longer mattered to me what others thought of my profession, so long as I liked it myself. I knew I'd undergo a collapse in social standing but I didn't care. I'd be going from *FT* columnist – with unreasonably high status – to teacher, where status is unreasonably low. In most of the world, according to research from the Varkey Foundation, teachers are seen as only a little ahead of police officers and far behind doctors and engineers. Only in a few places, like China, does society value the people who fill children's minds as highly as those who fix their bodies. Everywhere else, the sneery old saying still gets wheeled out: 'Those who can, do; those who can't, teach.'

But what happened to me was a surprise.

I didn't find that my status collapsed. The day after I'd written about becoming a teacher, I was flagged down on my bike on High Holborn by a middle-aged man who said: 'I think what you're doing is great.' From the start, people seemed interested in what I was up to. If status is what the *Cambridge Dictionary* says it is – 'the amount of respect, admiration or importance given to a person' – it was beginning to look like my status as a feeble novice teacher was higher than it had been as a columnist on one of the world's most respected publications.

One of my fellow trainees reported something similar. Louisa, a former top civil servant turned language teacher, noticed early on that people she met socially seemed far more interested in hearing about her new job than they ever were about her old one. Given that the low status of teachers is one of the reasons they are in such dangerously short supply, this glimpse of high status struck me as worth investigating.

So I did a survey of all the Now Teachers and asked them: Do people you meet at parties (assuming you still go to any) find you more interesting than before? Most confirmed they were too weary for socialising, but had noticed people in general seemed keener on talking to them than they used to be. This may not be that surprising, as almost everyone is interested in education, and even if they are not interested in hearing about the inequalities and social problems of the classroom, they love a bloody story from the front line. A child who is getting high in your lesson on 'purple drank', the mixture of Sprite and cough mixture that some rappers are addicted to, makes a better anecdote than the minutes of a board meeting.

I then asked the group what becoming a teacher had done to their status in the eyes of their peers. Most used to do jobs that society values (and pays) highly, and most were towards the top of their respective trees. Now all are at the bottom of a less prestigious tree. Despite this, two-thirds said they felt their status had gone up.

It seems that becoming a teacher in your 50s, especially when you've had a certain amount of success doing something else, is seen – quite unfairly – as more impressive than becoming a teacher straight from university. One Now Teacher told me that all his aging friends from the corporate world were starting to worry if their lives had been well spent and looked on his defection with admiration and a tinge of envy. The conclusion of this does not strike me as particularly fair, but Now Teachers get more respect for what they do compared to their most hard-working younger colleagues.

My survey was picked up by the *Today* programme, and I went on air early one morning to discuss it. I explained the results were a living embodiment of Maslow's hierarchy of needs – we had somehow emerged at the top, at the self-actualisation phase, and those below were looking up with some respect. I also pointed out the irony: the minute we think we've gone post-status, our status actually rises.

Nick Robinson, who was doing the interview, cut in briskly: 'So what you are talking about is basically a luxury for privileged older people.'

I snapped that in just ten minutes' time, before most journalists got out of bed, I would be on playground duty in the pouring rain. That wasn't luxury as I understood it.

'Point taken,' he said.

About a year after this, Now Teach got a boost from an even more unexpected quarter, Covid-19.

As the working world came to a virtual stop, furloughed or Zoomed, people started to wonder what were the things in life that really mattered. The conclusion, for many, was that teaching mattered, and maybe they should try it.

Every month in the pre-Covid era, we would hold an information evening for middle-aged professionals who wanted to know more about teaching. Usually about 50 turned up and sometimes fewer – which would send me into a panic about recruitment numbers. But once lockdown hit, over 150 people were regularly tuning into our Zoom events to listen to me holding forth from my study at home about how much I loved my new career.

Only I didn't love it then. I absolutely loathed teaching during lockdown. From the terrible day when we gathered around a computer screen in the maths office at school and watched Boris Johnson announce that schools were closing and that exams were cancelled, my job became hateful to me. I disliked recording lessons and posting them on Google Classroom, knowing that half the students – those very same ones who were already doing badly – would not be listening to them. I hated not being able to see my students. I hated the sterility of the technology, and even more how rubbish I was at using it. Sometimes I would record an entire lesson only to discover I'd pressed the wrong button and it hadn't recorded at all. My adult children, on their own Zoom calls elsewhere in the house, would sometimes hear the furious yelling of their mother: 'I FUCKING HATE THIS!'

Far more than my own incompetence, I hated the flattened voices of my students when I called them. A few barely got out of bed and seemed to have given up not just on work but on everything. If I was hardly coping in my large, light house, with my garden in which the damson blossom was ravishing, how were they coping in tiny flats?

I might have been lying when I said I was loving teaching, but I wasn't lying when I said teaching was more important than ever. Lockdown taught all of us – teachers, parents and students – something I hope we don't forget for a very long time. School is essential. It is there not only to teach, but to babysit, to socialise and to provide structure. Teenagers fared poorly without the routine and conviviality of school – and so did I.

In the Covid year, Now Teach ended up recruiting 150 people, its highest number ever. They were no longer exclusively the elite City types of the first year, but a broader bunch, teaching all subjects, and some of them, as far as I could tell from peering at my screen, were as impressive or more so than any of our past recruits. Every cloud has a silver lining and all that; the pandemic might have killed a couple of million people, but it proved a more effective Pied Piper in luring aging professionals towards the classroom than I'd ever been.

7

Hair

In June 2017, just before my 58th birthday, I stopped dying my hair brown. I let the grey roots grow as long as I could bear, had most of the coloured ends cut off and white streaks put through the rest of it. This was the final frontier. I'd done house, husband and job. It was time for hair.

Going grey should have been the most piffling change of all. The arguments in favour were unassailable. It cost over £100 every time I went to the hairdresser and involved spending the best part of a morning or afternoon trapped in a chair with tin foil on my head. Torching both money and time might have been sensible had the results been sufficiently pleasing, but even when straight from the hairdresser I was never entirely happy with the colour of my hair. It is one of the oddest failures of modern science that we can more or less build a human being in a Petri dish but no one has figured out how to make a brown hair dye that does not have a nasty tinge of either orange or green. This phoney brown was bad enough against my 40-something face, but as the years passed and as my skin proceeded on its journey towards parchment, the combination of hair and face became less and less prepossessing.

If I wasn't happy as I left the hairdresser, I became actively unhappy in the six weeks that followed. There would be a fortnight of looking reasonable followed by another month of looking increasingly less so, as the white margin inexorably widened along my parting. Sometimes I'd take matters into my own hands and do a DIY job, which had the advantage of taking ten minutes and costing £7, but the disadvantage of being blotchy, and resulting in a partially dyed bathroom.

So why did I, and why does almost every other woman I know, keep at it? The answer is so obvious that it's hardly worth writing. Because grey means old, and no one wants to be that.

When she was a mere 50, my mum – my model in so many things – went white. Until then she'd dyed her hair an olive-green colour, which was what passed for dark blonde in the 1960s, but on her 50th birthday she decided enough was enough. She went to the most expensive hairdresser in Mayfair, had it cut into a fashionably short crop (a bit like Judi Dench before her time), and thereafter was white-headed. Possibly she looked older; definitely she looked better.

On my 50th birthday there was no way on earth I was going to follow Mum. Then, I was frightened by the signs of age that had recently been advancing so precipitously. Until I was about 40, I looked a decade younger than I was, with round face and thin, childish body. As a 30-year-old, working for the *FT* in Brussels, I remember being introduced to the French head of press at the European Commission, who took one look at me and said: 'I didn't know the *Financial Times* employed children.' This was horrible, but when it stopped and people no longer marvelled at how young I looked, I hated that too. My formerly chubby cheeks were collapsing into loose jowls. I went seamlessly from hating looking young to hating looking old.

At about that time a friend persuaded me to go with her to a Harley Street clinic for a free Botox consultation. The doctor sat me down and explained that because my face was already very far gone I'd need untold syringes of Botox and filler to make a difference, and that I'd have to come back every few months for top-ups. She showed me a book of before-and-after pictures of her clients, most of whom had been rendered not so much young by her handiwork as peculiar. If this dodgy gallery was not enough to put me off, the women in the waiting room with their vacant faces and glossy Selfridges bags confirmed this was not for me.

As I cycled home, I realised the problem with Botox (apart from the fact that you look weird and can't smile) is that it's a psychologically flawed strategy, as it involves upping the ante in a battle you are always going to lose. The more you fight to look young, the more painful it is going to be when you inevitably don't. The only answer is to accept the fact that every year you look older than the year before – and not to mind.

My head knew this, but my heart said, 'No way: don't give up on the highlights.'

Nearly a decade later, galvanised by the other changes in my life, I consider the matter again. I'm sitting in the hairdresser's waiting for the brown dye to do its thing and really wishing it would hurry up as Katie and I have a meeting with a head teacher. I'm too preoccupied to do more than flick the pages of the glossy magazine in my lap, but then my eye lights on an article claiming grey hair is empowering for women. As if to prove it, Christine Lagarde and Helen Mirren stare out of the page, looking duly powerful. I examine them sceptically: Lagarde has olive skin and chic French clothes and pretty much runs the global economy and so is going to look formidable whatever her hair colour. Helen Mirren's hair doesn't persuade me either, partly because she must be well over 70 but also because she's Helen Mirren.

I show the article to my hairdresser who is now opening the folded foil attached to my head and peering inside to see if the colour has taken.

Me: Do you think I'd look good with grey hair?

Hairdresser: You'd hate it. Trust me.

Me: Are you sure?

Hairdresser: It would add ten years on you. You'd look totally washed out.

As she's not impartial in this matter, I canvass my friends. Don't do it, they all advise. But they are not impartial either, as most of them go to the hairdresser every month and part with over 100 quid in return for brown or blonde locks, or for locks any colour other than their natural grey. One day I have a conversation with a particularly good friend that goes like this.

Me: I'm thinking of going grey. Do you think I could carry it off?

Friend: Maybe – but not yet.

Me: Why not?

Friend: Well, if you're still doing internet dating ...?

Me (*prickly*): What's that got to do with it?

Friend: You're always complaining that men only want younger women—

Me: I'm not 'always complaining', and anyway, some men don't want younger women.

Friend: Yes, but if you use a picture of yourself with grey hair, that's not going to help, is it?

This exchange makes me so cross I snatch up the phone to make an appointment. If this really is the game – that a woman my age has to put chemicals on her hair to have any hope of finding a match among men who are themselves not only grey-haired but balding too – then I'm not playing. If any possible swain rules me out because I have grey hair, I'll rule him out as a moron.

Hair has always been an area of unfairness between the sexes. Men spend no time on theirs, and when it falls out or goes grey either no one cares or they get congratulated on becoming silver foxes. Women are expected to do time with the blow drier every day and then, as we get older, are chained to the dyeing treadmill. If we break rank and go grey we're seen as old bags, too ancient to be fanciable.

Men could possibly complain that some sexism runs the other way – a man who dyes his hair is seen by some people (including me) as insecure and an all-round figure of fun. I once went on a date with someone whose hair was a solid pancake of artificial brown. I wasn't that keen on him anyway, but for me the rich burgundy tones were a red line. I can see that this unequal treatment might be a bit unfair on men, but is surely minor compared to the follicle sexism that women have to bear.

My decision to go grey was an act of fuck-you defiance. For the first time in my life I was going to look the age I actually was. More than that, I was going to be fine with it. There is nothing shameful with being nearly 60, and if I also look nearly 60, what could be the conceivable problem with that?

The results were immediate – and far worse than I had expected. On my first trip to the Hackney Picturehouse with new grey hair I am asked by the man behind the counter: 'Will that be a seniors' ticket?' 'No!' I snap back, though my outrage is unreasonable as he was only jumping the gun by two years. On the train the next day a woman not much younger than me springs to her feet to offer me a seat. 'No thank you,' I say icily. 'I can stand.'

My pupils, who never knew me in my brown-haired incarnation, are in no doubt that I am ancient. One day during my training year I show my Year 7s a copy of the *FT* with a picture of me taken a year and a half earlier with dyed hair on the masthead. Most don't recognise me. One sharp-eyed 12-year-old shouts out: 'Aww, Miss, is that you? Is that when you was young?'

On another occasion I set the class a worded problem of the sort they find hard. Lenny is 12 and I am five times his age. How old am I? One boy put up his hand, skipping the mental maths and going straight for the most likely answer: 85?

The public reaction was not what I was hoping for but I have learnt not to care. I am not displeased when I look in the mirror, and actively like the defiant look in my eye. It says: This is what I look like – do you have a problem with that? Although objectively I look worse than I ever have, in my subjective universe something odd has happened that leaves me feeling happier about my appearance than I used to. This is a miracle of aging that no one ever told me about: though my skin has sagged, my expectations have sagged even more. To the grey reflection that stares back at me, I say: you're not too bad, given everything.

While my face, my body and my hair look older, an odd thing is happening to my clothes, which are marching off in the opposite direction. Today I'm wearing jeans in this year's cut, with a very high waist and wide legs, bought online by my daughter. She had rejected them as not sufficiently flattering and I claimed them myself.

Me: Do I look silly in these?
Rose: No, you look great!
Me: Are you sure?
Rose: For God's sake, Mum. Yes.

Rose is a first-born and a people-pleaser, but either way, I like them. I'm wearing them now.

My wardrobe is more of a muddle than it's ever been, possibly reflecting the new, untoward stage in my life. When I was a student I wore student clothes, jeans and Fair Isle jumpers I'd knitted myself. In the early part of my professional life I dressed like the scruffy journalist and mother I was. I was too tired to think about clothes much and spent very little money on them. In my mid-40s I was appointed a non-executive director of a big insurance company and spent some of the extra cash on expensive corporate suits. At one point I paid £680 for a Paul Smith dress – which I suppose was vaguely justifiable in that I wore it to every corporate do and for every speech I gave for three years. Measured by price-per-wear it wasn't too bad. Now I look back at such expenditure with mild disapproval. It's not only more than half my take-home monthly pay but seems morally dubious to spend so much money on a scrap of wool, polyester and spandex.

Now I'm surrounded by young teachers I find I'm slowly drifting towards wearing what they do. The black leather handbag I carried every day for a decade has been replaced by a yellow canvas backpack. Almost everything I've bought in the last couple of years comes from eBay – and because hardly anything I buy costs more than a tenner, I can take risks. A few months ago I bought some wet-look lace-up boots, very chunky, with a platform sole, that I got for £5. They attracted various compliments at morning briefing on their first outing to school, and I was feeling pretty good until the heel of one of them detached itself during a lesson – meaning I had to teach for half an hour frozen to the spot, and at break I had to borrow a pair of a colleague's shoes and nip round the corner to buy some Super Glue.

One January day, a bit over a year into my new life, I went into a clothes shops in Dalston where there was a sale on, and spotted a baggy boiler suit made of chunky scarlet corduroy. When I was a teenager, all my coolest friends wore men's boiler suits, mostly bought from Laurence Corner, the army surplus shop on Hampstead Road. But whenever I tried them

I'd find even the smallest size so vast on my puny body, so I always went home empty-handed.

I took the red boiler suit to the changing room, tried it on, and emerged uncertainly into the shop where the cool assistants swore it looked great on me.

'You can *so* carry that off,' one of them insisted.

I got her to take a picture which I posted on our family WhatsApp. David replied first.

Hmm. Not sure red is your colour.

I ignored this just as I'd ignored his wardrobe advice for a quarter of the century, and waited for the children. Presently Stan replied.

So cool! haha. defs buy it.

I needed no further encouragement. I handed over £80 for the red suit and skipped out of the shop. The last time I'd been this happy with new clothes I was ten and had come home from school to find my mum had been to Kids in Gear in Carnaby Street and bought me a black chunky cord mini-skirt with a wide red belt, which, now I think of it, was similar to this new buy half a century later.

My glee was slightly dented on the boiler suit's first outing when I wore it on a date with a man I'd met online. He seemed untroubled by the grey hair but drew the line at my outfit, which he said would be just the thing to wear to a *Super Mario* fancy-dress party. I have banished this memory (as well as the man) and have returned to basking in the harmless and unexpected pleasure at having something in my wardrobe that was denied me 45 years earlier.

The boiler suit represents something that pleases me. All my life I have dressed either to fit in or to look attractive or to look powerful. Looking back, I don't think I ever managed to look any of these things particularly successfully and so it is thrilling to discover that I'm no longer trying to look anything in particular. These days, for the first time in six decades, I dress only to please myself.

8

One Day

6.25am

The alarm goes off, but I'm not asleep. I am three years into teaching and on this November morning, as on most others, I wake early, braced for the day to come. My clothes from yesterday lie on the bathroom floor. I would put them straight back on, but don't for fear of what my students might think – I don't want them to conclude Miss Kellaway is dirty as well as being a bit weird. I put on the same trousers and boots but find a different shirt and jacket.

Downstairs, Rose is getting last night's leftovers out of the fridge and putting them into two Tupperware boxes – one for her and one for me.

Rose: What have you got on today?
Me: Double with my Year 10s first thing, but I'm not well prepared …
Rose: It'll be OK. You'll be amazing.

*

Rose is 29 and, apart from the fact that she is briefly living with me until she can get the money together to buy a flat, is a fully functioning adult. In some ways I am still a regular mother in that I worry she works too hard and that the batteries on her bike lights haven't been charged, yet professionally our roles have reversed. She has been a teacher for seven years to my three. She has taught in a variety of places, some very difficult indeed, and is paid 80 per cent more than I am. She is my mentor, my cheerleader, my teacher.

6.53am

The walk from my house to school takes exactly 21 minutes at a brisk pace. The route goes through a churchyard and under a railway bridge where a pile of dirty bedding mainly covers two sleeping bodies. It smells of pee. Today it is raining and still dark.

7.14am

I open the heavy gate at the side of the school with a pass that hangs on a green lanyard round my neck. The clock inside tells me I'm 14 minutes later than I'd planned.

I cross the AstroTurfed green and go into the old Victorian building, and up a secret back staircase forbidden to students to where eight maths, economics and business studies teachers share a cramped office.

I start going through my email and check the Daily Bulletin at the top of my inbox. This is written by the shaven-headed chief disciplinarian in the school and informs me that I'm covering a Year 8 registration for a teacher who is absent – which means I've lost 20 valuable minutes between 8.20 and 8.40 – and that one of my Year 10 students has been excluded for a week so I need to take work for him to the office. No reason is given – it is a constant disappointment to me that we are never told what outrageous thing our students are supposed to have done. I photocopy two pages of a textbook and put a Post-it note on the top saying: 'Read, take notes and do q5.'

I need to print the classwork for the first two periods, but the printer is jammed – again. Cursing, I go down to the library and wait while a geography teacher prints out what seems to be an entire atlas and then busies herself with the guillotine, cutting the margins off so that they will stick neatly into students' books. I print my sheets and take them back upstairs where I start hacking at the margins with a pair of blunt children's scissors.

7.58am

'Briefing!' says the best organised of my colleagues. She is 24, younger than all but one of my children, and a model of professional behaviour. Last week she gave me a 'shout-out' card, which teachers are encouraged to give each other to keep up morale. She'd written in it: 'Thanks for being a constant source of entertainment' – which I think she meant nicely.

We file down the narrow stairs and past the school gates, where there is a crowd of kids waiting to be let in on the dot of 8am.

'How was your date with that guy you were going to meet?' one of my maths teacher friends asks me as we walk. 'Grim,' I say. She laughs.

I have been at this school for two years, and though I'm firm friends with my immediate colleagues I barely know the names of many of the other teachers. My school, like most academies, has no general staffroom – probably because the managers fear that if teachers spend too much time sitting around with cups of tea they'll start to moan.

7.59am

We are almost running as we approach the auditorium – you get told off if you are ten seconds late for briefing – but today our urgency is heightened by the weekly gift of a free pastry. I am just in time for the last clammy pain au chocolat – leaving the people behind me with no choice but the frosted cinnamon swirls.

8am

A slide on the giant screen in the auditorium reads:

> *DO NOW: What is the difference between extrinsic and intrinsic cognitive load?*

I have a dim memory of an earlier training session with this detail in it, but my own cognitive load is so excessive right now the only thing that would relieve it would be some extra time to plan my Year 10 lesson. Instead we get a five-minute blast from a RE teacher whose title is 'Excellent Teacher' (the implication being that the rest of us are Rubbish Teachers) on how to break our explanations down to make them easier to understand.

The training 'nugget' is followed by notices. X in Year 10 has been diagnosed with epilepsy – all staff must familiarise themselves with what to do if he has a fit. Y and Z must not be allowed to sit next to each other or talk to each other in the playground. And on it goes.

There are 780 students in this school. We are in loco parentis to them not just collectively but as individual children. This is both impressive and impossible: I don't teach the epileptic boy but already know I won't get around to finding the note about him on the system. There just isn't time.

8.13am

Teachers are released into the playground where line-up is beginning. Students hurry towards their form groups, inserting themselves into the correct alphabetical slot in the line. Before the bell has gone, a silence falls that is so complete I close my eyes and fancy myself alone in the playground. My colleagues are moving up and down the lines, checking uniforms.

I head for where the Year 8s congregate, next to the basketball hoops. 'Hands out of pockets,' I say to a 12-year-old boy. This is not my favourite part of the job, but the head teacher is glaring at me and so I make a perfunctory effort. My own hands are in my pockets and I briefly take them out, but then find the air so cold I put them back in again.

I have forgotten to check which room I'm in for registration – which last year would have thrown me into a panic, but now I tell the girl at the front of the line to lead off and I tag along behind her, with the air of someone who knows what they are about.

8.20am

Thirty 12-year-olds file into a Victorian classroom and stand silently behind their desks. 'Good morning, Year 8,' I say. 'Good morning, Miss Kellaway,' they reply, in perfect unison.

At the beginning I found this scarily robotic, but now I'm soothed by the routine and grateful for the silence. School life is intrinsically so chaotic that this sort of certainty has something to be said for it. The pupils know exactly what they are meant to do all day, starting with 20 minutes silent reading during reception, followed by six orderly lessons of 55 minutes each.

I take the register and go round the class to check weekly planners have been signed by parents, and then sign them myself. One girl has forgotten to get her parent to sign, a crime for which I should have given a detention, but instead I whisper: 'Get it done tonight.'

8.39am

'Pack up,' I say. They put their planners and books into their backpacks. I stand at the door. 'Goodbye,' I say to them. 'Have a nice day.'

'Have a nice day, Miss,' they reply.

8.40am

Upstairs my Year 10 economics students have formed a line outside my classroom. 'Good morning, Amala; good morning, Harry; good morning, Titilayo,' I say as they file in. I have been teaching this class longest and even though I'm not supposed to have favourite students, these are the ones I like best. A hulk of a 15-year-old comes lumbering in.

Me: Good morning, Demarcus.
Demarcus (*muttering and looking at the ground*): Morning.

Me: Look at me, please, Demarcus, when you say good morning. Do it again.

Second time he complies, just about.

Two of the students are loitering outside the door because they don't want me to pounce on them and ask them about the news. I tell them to come in, and as they unpack their books, I pounce on one of them.

'What's happening in the world, Patrick?'

This is how every lesson begins: I pick on a couple of kids as they stand behind their desks and they have to tell me an economics news story – or else they get a detention. Just as the school forces students to tuck in shirts, I have elected to force them to engage with the world.

Patrick (*looking briefly panicked*): Er, Chelsea has a new manager.

Me: That's not an economics story.

I confiscate his planner, with a view to adding a detention in it. Dalmar puts his hand up.

'It is, Miss. It's economics because if the football team is more successful, the club may employ more people, and that will have an effect on unemployment.'

I laugh, give him an achievement mark, and return Patrick's planner to him.

I wait for perfect silence and then begin:

'Throughout this lesson … ' This is the cue every teacher must give at start of every class, triggering the recital of a secular prayer. The children generally produce a dirge so lowering that I have taken to leading the recital myself, setting a cracking pace.

' … I aspire to maintain an enquiring mind, a calm disposition and an attentive ear so that in this class and in all classes I can fulfil my true potential.'

As we speed-chant, I walk down the aisle in the centre of my long classroom, meeting the eye of every student to make sure they are saying it properly, and also to send the message: I'm in charge here. Don't even think of trying anything.

'Thank you. Sit down.'

I then tell them the news story I want to talk about. 'Denise Coates, the CEO of Bet365, earned 323 MILLION pounds last year.'

The class gasps.

In my old life, I tried to avoid writing about excessive executive pay as there was nothing interesting to say about it, save that it was excessive. It is particularly so when compared to the likely household income of half my students who are on free school meals.

Me: Does Coates deserve the money?

Umit: Yeah, she deserves it.

Me: Don't call out. Why does she deserve it?

Umit: Because she worked hard.

Me: But cleaners also work hard, and they get minimum wage.

Umit (*giving me a pitying look*): She must have studied hard at school to get where she is. She has made the company successful so she should keep the money herself.

Me: But if you were a lowly worker at Bet365 and your bosses made 5,000 times as much as you did, how would you feel?

Bismark raises his hand. 'It would make me work harder, so I can get to her position.'

In a way it's cheering that these students believe so passionately that if they work hard the world will be theirs. Yet as their teacher, I wonder if I should introduce a note of reality and tell them that in real life, the spoils sometimes get divided not by hard work but by luck, by power and by vested interest.

At this point the head teacher, who is a good two decades my junior and has been in education all his life, drifts in. This is unfortunate. Fifteen minutes of the lesson have gone and not only have I not yet taught them a single thing on the curriculum, we haven't even done the starter. Their purple exercise books are not open. I explain we've had a bit of a diversion into executive pay and he gives an inscrutable nod.

For all its strictness, the school does give some latitude to teachers on how they teach. Yet this is provisional, and puts the onus on me. I need to prove that I can get good results – and I have absolutely no idea if I can. Is it possible to teach both the world and the syllabus? If not, is there a trade-off? If children get one grade lower because they have spent a lot of time thinking about broader things, how much does it matter?

8.56am

I put my hand to my head and encounter a lump tangled in my hair. It is a silicone ear plug that must have fallen out in the night. I put the starter questions on the board and when students' heads are bowed, remove the offending lump and put it in my pocket.

> *What is the basic economic problem?*
> *What is derived demand?*
> *Draw what happens to the market for nurses when government spending on the health service increases.*

I enjoy writing these questions, designed to assess how much students can remember of what they're supposed to have learnt from earlier lessons. I like it even more when peace falls around the class as they all write the title of today's class and the date and get to work.

No matter how often they go through this ritual they never complain. They turn out to like routine, which shouldn't be such a shock to me given how much I like it myself.

I go around the class, looking over shoulders and chivvying.

'Why haven't you even started, Bismark? Too slow, Harris! Achievement point for the first to finish with all correct answers! Umit is already on question four!'

One kid who always finishes first puts up his hand. I glance at his scrawl. 'Question three is wrong. Try again.'

When I started teaching I marvelled at the way teachers could look at an exercise book and spot a mistake before their eyes had even had time to focus. Now, three years in, miraculously and inexplicably, I can do this too.

A second puts up his hand. There are more mistakes there, too, but it's better than his usual effort. I give the achievement mark to him, ignoring cries of 'Aww, Miss!' and return to my desk to write his name on a scrap of paper. Who did I give a mark to earlier? I try to think and remember it was Dalmar. I scribble his name down too.

The principal is now inspecting the children's books. He is checking to see that homework has been set every six lessons, that it has been thoroughly marked, that students have written corrections in green pen, and that I've marked the corrections. This is an impossibly onerous requirement, one that I try to meet, but often don't quite manage.

I offer up a prayer that the books he's looking at are in order. If not, I'll be summoned later to be told my marking is not up to scratch. He walks out of the class, and I feel instantly lighter.

9.20am

Belatedly, I start Unit 2.2.1: 'The Role of Financial Markets'. According to the course, there are three sorts of financial institution: banks, building societies and insurance companies. Having spent three decades on the *Financial Times*, I disapprove of this arbitrary simplification, but go along with it, more or less.

I show them a picture of the City of London.

Me: Where is this?

Alice: New York.

(*Various kids laugh mockingly, which is my cue to go fake mad*)

Me: I will not have ANYONE laughing at wrong answers in my class!

Demarcus's shoulders are still shaking. I remove his planner.

Only half the students can identify the picture as London. None has heard the phrase 'City of London' or knows what or where it is, despite the fact the Bank of England is barely three miles from where they are sitting.

I start to go through the slides explaining the three sorts of institution and what they do. Almost none of these 15-year-olds can tell me what a mortgage is or explain how insurance works. I tell them that for nine years I was on the board of a car insurance company, and explain that if you crash into someone's car and make them quadriplegic and unable to work, your insurer has to pay their medical bills for the rest of their life and also their forgone earnings. The biggest payout during my years was £9 million. The class listens agog. A forest of hands goes up.

Umit: Miss, basically, like—
Me: Start again, please, without a 'basically' or a 'like'.
Umit: Yeah, well, why can't I just pretend to have an accident and get £9 million?

This student always can be depended on to weigh in if there is a possibility of a scam. Which leads to an interesting discussion on insurance fraud.

Now back to the definitions.

An insurance company is a financial institution that guarantees compensation for a specified loss, damage, illness or death in return for an agreed premium.

They copy this into their books, the quick ones having to wait for the ones who write painfully slowly. Then we move through the other institutions.

10.07am

I hand out the work I printed earlier, a list of questions and a table drawing on what they have supposedly learnt today.

There is barely 20 minutes of the class left, which isn't enough. They should be working alone for longer than this.

I look over the shoulder of one student, who is writing 'the role of insurance companies is to give millions to people who crash their cars'.

'Pens down.'

All but three or four students comply. I stand perfectly still with eyes boring into the students who are still writing. This is a trick I have recently mastered after two years trying. By some magic I don't entirely understand, they stop and put their pens down.

I tell them again what an insurance company does, repeating that car insurance is only a small part of it. They return to filling in the sheets.

10.28am

'Start packing up.' As they do so, I start a barrage of questions: 'What's a medium of exchange, Sarah? What's an insurance company, Olly?' I have learnt to say the name after the question. If you say it first, the rest of the class switches off as it doesn't concern them.

A girl at the front puts up her hand.

Nadia: What's for homework, Miss?
Me (*talking slowly to hide the fact that I have quite forgotten and need to think something up on the hoof*): Homework is to

google HSBC. Find ten different services they offer customers – mortgages, savings accounts – and write a paragraph explaining each. Due next Wednesday.

Students make hasty notes in their planners. This is terrible homework: it's not on the curriculum, it's poorly explained, and it's an opportunity for the ten brightest students to do some interesting research, and for everyone else to do some indiscriminate copying off the internet. Too bad.

10.31am

The bell has gone for morning break. Everyone has left apart from Demarcus. Skulking outside are two others to whom I gave detentions yesterday for coming to school without their books.

Demarcus is looking aggrieved. For this sullen body language alone, I should increase the sanction.

Demarcus: I wasn't the only one laughing.
Me: But you were the only one not to stop when I told you to.

To each of my detainees I give a 'Rule, Reason, Response' sheet, on which they must describe their misdemeanour, explain what was wrong about it, and how they propose to avoid doing something similar in the future.

10.43am

I release them all into the playground two minutes early as I have to deliver the work for the excluded student and I need to pee.

It is only since becoming a teacher I have understood the joy of going to the loo at work. You get to lock yourself into a solitary space where the only disturbance is other teachers rattling at the door trying to get in. If you are lucky, as I am now, the disabled loo is free, which is huge and has its own basin in it. I wash my hands and luxuriate under the blower until they are dry.

10.50am

Outside the students have lined up again and are filing into lessons. I now have a double free period, the first of which is partly taken up with a weekly meeting with my HOLA (Head of Learning Area) who teaches computer science. We are not a natural pair. I don't think he has ever met anyone as bad with computers as I am, but I have never met anyone who likes putting data into spreadsheets as much as he does. I present myself at the door of his tiny office.

Chris: Alright, Luce? How's it going?
Me: Excellent.

I have learnt that any admission that things are not great will result in my having to fill in another spreadsheet.

'Let's start with Year 11,' he says. 'What interventions are you planning?'

This class, which will sit their GCSEs in the summer, is not looking good. Each student has a target grade, an official projection based on their scores when they left primary school. This grade is the benchmark against which the government measures the value added by schools – and schools measure the value added by teachers.

My school is among the 100 best schools in the country; to hold on to its position each student must on average get at least a grade higher than their targets. In my class many of the students are three or four whole grades below their targets. Romeo is meant to get a 9 but is now on a 3.

'The same as last week. I'm setting a lot of homework. I'm focusing very tightly on the syllabus. I'm doing mixed tests at the beginning of every lesson. I'm giving extra classes after school once a week. I am making sure they learn all the key terms.'

He nods, types some information into his computer and tells me to phone parents of underperformers. He instructs me to fill in a spreadsheet of the students whose parents I've called.

Chris: How are you getting on with Google Classroom? I need you to upload all your lessons onto it.

Me: I'm afraid I haven't done anything. I'm too busy, and I can't remember how to use it.

*

I feel a bit sorry for him having to manage me. I am a tricky mixture of inexperience and overconfidence – and have started querying policies that I don't agree with. For the first year I kept my head down and did (more or less) what I was told. Now I'm borderline disobedient.

The upshot of the meeting is that he gets to tick me off the long to-do list on his iPad, while I get to be even more worried about my Year 11s than I was before, and now have to make some difficult calls to parents.

11.15am

Back at my desk I check my emails and find an officious message, copied to Chris, telling me off for having failed to take the register in the last lesson. Damn. I was thrown off track by the appearance of the principal.

I take the register retrospectively and then turn to the pile of purple exercise books from my worrying Year 11 class.

Evaluate the effect of a rise in the value of the pound on UK consumers.

Romeo's book is on the top. I see his chaotic writing on the front, sigh and slot the book further down the pile, and open the next one. This belongs to a hard-working girl who has written a page and a half in beautiful round script.

The effect of a rise in the pound is that consumers buy less from abroad because it's more expensive.

'God,' I groan out loud. 'They don't bloody understand it! I spent the entire sodding lesson explaining this!'

Two of my colleagues look up from their marking and make sympathetic noises. The next few books are better. I circle spelling mistakes and write 'Good!' in the margin a lot.

11.45am

The bell goes. I'm meant to be on 'transition duty' on the other side of the site and I hurry over, a bit late. Two girls are whispering to each other.

Me (*yelling in faux indignation*): Why are you talking? [I know exactly why they are talking: because they are children and because they have something to say to their friends.]
Girls: Sorry, Miss.

Back in my office I tackle the book of a Year 11 student I'm particularly worried about. Tyreece has written barely half a page, has neglected to make a single accurate point about anything, and has not even attempted half the questions. I write 'D' for 'detention', and call his mother.

I can hear the fall in her voice when I introduce myself.

Me: I'm Tyreece's new economics teacher, and I'm a little worried about him. His last homework was incomplete and poorly answered – he's not doing his best.

Tyreece's mother: With respect, I'm sick and tired of teachers saying Reece isn't trying. He used to love economics with the old teacher, but now, no offence, he doesn't like it anymore.

Me: Yes, but either way he has an exam to sit in seven months. I'm here to help, but I can't do that if he doesn't try. If things don't improve the three of us must have a meeting.

I put down the phone feeling offended. I doubt if the call has cheered her, either.

I finish my marking and enter all the grades into an old-fashioned paper register that I am hiding from my manager. I know I should put them into the system, but paper is quicker. The grades tell me what I already know. About half the students have a reasonable understanding of exchange rates. Half do not. But then half are reasonably able, and half are less so. What am I supposed to do about this? Do I spend more time going over it, when there is so much else we haven't covered? I wish I knew.

I turn my attention to the afternoon's lessons. Today I teach two Year 9 classes one after another, which means only one lesson to plan, given twice over.

I enjoy planning lessons but it strikes me as a shocking waste of time. Why aren't there national lesson plans designed by the best teachers in the country and updated every year? I spend the next 20 minutes hastily scrabbling around for material and putting together a slap-dash PowerPoint.

12.28pm

There are ten minutes until lunchbreak and I must eat now as I'm on duty – it is four and a half hours since the pastry and I am ravenously hungry. I put the Tupperware box in the microwave but the machine is so old and slow I give up after a minute of watching it go round and return to my desk with a plastic box of cold lentils that are warmish around the edges. I eat them at speed, dropping a forkful into a student's open book as I do so.

12.40pm

For the first half of lunchtime I'm stationed on the green. Today it is drizzling, but not enough for the students to be inside. I'm in a big puffa coat with a hood, but hardly any of the kids, and none of the boys, wear coats. I watch them stand around in the damp talking and laughing in groups while I hover on my own, bored and cold. I'm pleased when a student approaches, his eyes shining.

'Miss, I saw an article you wrote.'

I don't ask which one but fear the worst – that an article I wrote about dating is doing the rounds.

Me: Quite possible. I used to be a journalist. Are you interested in journalism?
Student: Nah.

He wanders off to giggle with his friends.

A Year 8 boy who took part in a debate I arranged comes up to discuss the election. He wants to be a politician.

Me: Do you like Boris Johnson?
Student: No. He's a liar. But I still think this country needs someone like him.

Over his shoulder I see a large group of students congregating. The school only allows up to eight students to talk together, but this is a cluster of ten smallish boys. I tell them two of them must leave the group, and stand there looking fierce until, reluctantly, a pair peels away.

1.05pm

For the second half of duty I'm stationed in the canteen queue. Some of the students I teach in Year 11 are queuing up.

Me: Brilliant homework, Benjamin. I'm going to ring your mum.

Noah: Will you ring *my* mum?

Me: Yes – to tell her you don't work hard enough.

Student chorus: Ooooh, Noah! You've been violated!

In the canteen, students are eating curry and rice with a despised side of broccoli. For pudding it's fruit or cake, but no one has fruit. As I stand there, directing students with trays, I remember with a lurch that the slides for that afternoon's lesson are still open on my computer back in the office, which means I won't be able to get at them in the classroom. I can't leave my duty. But equally I can't teach the next lesson without my slides. I decide to make a dash for it, sprinting up the back stairs, saving and closing the presentation, and running back downstairs, heart thudding as much from danger as from exertion.

The lead duty supervisor didn't notice. Phew. It is strange to find myself at the age of 60 living for the first time in my life under a disciplinary regime.

1.35pm

The children start to line up in the playground. It's the same thing. Bags down, silence. Class by class they are called.

The head of Year 9 bellows, 'If you have Miss Kellaway for economics, step to your right, go to the back, and form a line in front of Miss Kellaway.

Twenty-five 13-year-olds comply and I lead an orderly crocodile up to my classroom.

One of them has come to class with a sophisticated news story about the US–China trade war. I award her an achievement point. Another reads out a story word for word copied from the BBC website, evidently not understood at all.

We rattle through the reflection, they sit down, and I put the starter questions on the board. While they work, I take the register. It feels orderly and purposeful.

What causes a contraction in demand?
Which factor of production is a fish?

And so on.

Most of them are getting the questions right. I used to think that asking kids things they already knew was pointless. But it's not: it puts them in a good mood for learning new things.

And then we start on the topic of the day: elasticity of demand.

'Sit up, Matthew.' Matthew is my brightest student, who would be a pleasure to teach if he weren't so arrogant he thinks sitting properly is beneath him.

He sits up with effort, and we begin. I ask the class to consider two items: petrol and Mars Bars. Imagine the price of each doubled. We know that demand would fall, but by how much?

They discuss this in pairs. Each stronger child has been paired with a weaker one. Most of them get the idea that demand for petrol is not very price elastic – demand doesn't fall much when the price doubles. But most think that demand for Mars isn't elastic either.

> Me: Look. If Mars Bars in the local sweet shop are £1.60 instead of 80p most people will buy Snickers instead.
> (*A lot of sceptical faces.*)
> Abdul: I won't – I don't like Snickers!
> Benjamin: Snickers is WAY better than Mars.
> Emmanuel: No way!!!

This has the makings of a riot, so I shut it down firmly.

'In economics, what do we call pairs of goods like Mars and Snickers?'

Many hands go up, but I pick on Hamil whose hand is not up and who is a weak student who has been in trouble recently.

He looks baffled but after considerable prompting supplies the right answer: substitute goods. 'Fantastic!' I gush, as if to a genius. 'Well done!'

I then ask them to draw the demand curves. This takes a while, and a lot of modelling from me. I have lost my board rubber, so have to keep wiping the board with my sleeve.

I set them to work to come up with ten products that have price-elastic demand and ten that don't.

Each pair supplies an example to the class and we discuss the reasons. This is the sort of thing that can either go well or be a shambles. Today, most of the students are on task and are supplying decent examples.

Someone brings up taxi rides.

'Gosh! That's fascinating!!!'

Two of the boys exchange amused glances – they think it's funny that Miss gets so excited about elasticity of demand. I let it pass.

It gives me the perfect link to my next slide: Uber's surge pricing. I ask them if they think Uber's consumers are more price conscious during the day or in the evening.

All the usual kids have their hands up. I ignore them and pick Elsie, a shy girl who works hard and hardly ever speaks. Only a third of my pupils are girls – and I try to make sure that all of their voices are heard.

Elsie answers: 'People are less price conscious in the evening because there are fewer substitutes like buses and trains, so the elasticity of demand is lower.'

This is a perfect answer. I congratulate her and give her an achievement point.

2.30pm

The bell goes; I collect their books as they go out.

As a journalist I was only ever as good as my last article. As a teacher it's the same. I'm as good as my last lesson. This one went well – it was a hard subject and they mostly got it – with the result that I'm left elated, and inclined to conclude that I've entirely cracked teaching.

But it's not over: my second Year 9 class is already waiting and I must go through the whole thing again.

Me: Good afternoon, Darius.
Chaquille: I'm not Darius.
Me: So sorry, Chaquille! I know perfectly well who you are – I'm just losing my marbles.

He doesn't know the phrase and gawps. It's a bad start.

We do the same lesson – only this time it is completely different. It should be better because I know I must head off the inevitable Mars versus Snickers war and be tighter on timing, but this advantage is outweighed by something much bigger. It is the last period of the day and students invariably become about five years less mature in period 6 than they were an hour earlier. We go through the same material, but they are flagging and so am I. At the end I am no longer elated: I feel like a failure.

3.25pm

The final bell goes. I have not sat down since 12.40. I am hoarse. I have no idea how three hours can have gone so quickly.

Now my time is theoretically my own, which means I can go to the loo and then start marking 50 Year 9 books. They have done their demand graphs well, which is a relief. I skim through as quickly as I can, but don't get far.

I look at my email: no bollocking email from the principal which means the books he checked must have been OK. No news is good news.

3.42pm

Outside the office one of my students is asking for me.

It is Beccy, a sweet Year 11 girl to whom economics is a scary land of alien ideas none of which she understands. I take her to an empty classroom and we sit side by side, and I try to explain exchange rates to her really slowly. By the end of half an hour she can tell me that a strong pound is generally good for UK consumers, which makes me want to whoop with joy. Whether she will still know that tomorrow is anyone's guess.

4.18pm

I haven't properly prepared my lessons for tomorrow, and I've still got 40 books left to mark. I go through the motions, doing just enough to avoid getting into trouble. I time myself: 2 minutes per book.

I've received an email asking for a report on a student I teach who is in trouble. I put this off and instead search on the system for the phone number of Elsie's mum.

English is not her first language, so I explain slowly.

Me: Your daughter is working so hard and is turning into a wonderful economist.

Elsie's mum (*voice breaking as if she's going to cry*): Thank you, bless you, thank you.

I put down the phone feeling happy. I resolve to make a call like this every day.

5.10pm

I mark a few more books and start looking at my Year 11 lesson plan for tomorrow. It's a mess. Too much copying from slides and not enough tasks. My head feels as if my brain has been removed and replaced with a lump of Blu Tack. It is telling me I must go home. At the start of this year I made a pact with Rose that teaching must be sustainable, which means I will not take any work home with me – not today and not ever. I will get in an hour earlier tomorrow to plan the lessons.

I start to pack up but then realise I haven't entered the day's detentions and achievement points into the central system. I hunt around for the scraps of paper I wrote them on but no luck. I enter some names into the system more or less at random. It will have to do.

5.40pm

I put on my coat and get my bag.

> Me: Bye, don't work too late.
> Other teachers: Bye, have a good evening.

I do the same walk as this morning in reverse, but more slowly. It is dark again. I'm exhausted, but not especially stressed. This is something odd about my new life: even though it is far more tiring than my old one, it doesn't stress me out in quite the same way. I think this is because it's not actually about me. It's about the students. I go over the day as I walk: I did some bad things and some good things. And that, it seems to me, is good enough.

6.02pm

I get home and dump my coat on the counter, as the extra energy required in hanging it up does not seem worth it.

6.03pm

I take the cork out of last night's red wine and pour myself a large glass. I open a packet of Kettle Chips and eat and drink standing up.

6.45pm

My daughter gets in.

> Rose: How was your day?
> Me: Not bad, but I had a slightly difficult conversation
> with the mother of one of my worst Year 11 students—
> Rose (*interrupting*): Mum, let's not talk about school
> stuff?

She has spent ten hours at the coal face in a much tougher
school than mine. And now she wants some life. I, on the
other hand, am still new enough to teaching and still so in
thrall to the whole thing, I don't want any other life at all.

I hold my peace, and we have supper and watch something
on Netflix instead.

9.05pm

I take my clothes off, dropping them on the floor, and get into
a hot bath.

9.20pm

Bed.

9

Just Be Happy, Darling

June 1977

I am sitting in the gym at school about to begin the last paper of my English A level. My head aches and I feel sick. At the back of my throat is the burn of stale alcohol.

The invigilator is telling us to write our names and the name of the school on the front of the paper. I can do the first, but the second is harder. 'Camden School for Grils', I write. This is not a good start to an English A level: I am aware of that.

I can't remember anything else about that paper. I can't remember whether the questions were on *Bleak House* and *King Lear* (good) or *Lyrical Ballads* and Milton (dreary). I can't even remember if, given the state I was in, I managed to write anything at all. But I do remember a surprising amount of what happened the night before.

I had gone out with my boyfriend's father. We had been to the theatre and then out to dinner, after which he had hailed a taxi in Soho in the small hours and bundled me into it. As he did so, he took his shoes off, thrust them into the cab with me and waved me off, standing in the gutter in his socks.

I'd met Matt at the beginning of my Upper Sixth year at a party. He was wearing a black leather biker's jacket and was already on a gap year before going to Cambridge. I adored him – and Mum was keen on him too, though mainly because his dad was an actor who she'd once seen playing Hamlet.

A few months after I'd met him, Matt took off for a six-month tour of South America. His dad and I went to see him off at Heathrow and on the way back he stopped to buy me a consolatory bunch of freesias. Once home, I threw the flowers on the hall floor and flung myself down beside them to howl into the dusty Persian rug. A week or so later I was still slouching around, comatose with grief, and Mum decided it was time for me to snap out of it. Only she didn't say that exactly: instead she opened her book of William Blake poems that Dad had given her for her birthday.

He who binds to himself a joy
Doth the winged life destroy.
He who kisses joy as it flies
Lives in eternity's sun rise.

I did not find this even slightly comforting. William Blake, I concluded, can't have ever been in love or he'd have known that when you love someone you don't wave them off with a kiss when they are about to leave you for six whole months; you lie on the floor and scream.

In June, a few weeks before Matt was due back, his father got in touch inviting me to a first night in the West End and dinner with the actors afterwards. Never mind the fact I had an A level exam the next day, Mum encouraged me to go.

She was still up when I came crashing home late and drunk. She didn't tell me off, she was too amused by the shoes – handmade suede brogues – which Matt's father had given to me as a sign that his son would return safely to fill them.

In the middle of August a brown envelope dropped through the door telling me that I'd got a C in my English A level. It would have been handy to blame this on my drunken night out, but my other grades told a different story: a B in maths (my strongest subject) and an O level pass in French, with a sublimely poor U for 'unclassified' in the oral.

Before the arrival of the envelope, Matt, who himself had four As, had often told me I was the cleverest person he'd ever met. Confronted with this new evidence he instantly revised his opinion and said: you are clever – but in an intuitive kind of way. I took this reappraisal even harder than I took the grades themselves.

Mum, on the other hand, did not see fit to change her view of me. Dad gave me a hug and said everything would be all right. Neither said the obvious thing: it serves you right for not working.

What interests me now is that neither of my parents did anything to prevent the car crash that was bound to happen. They never gave me nagging speeches about how it mattered to get good grades. Mum never once told me to do my homework – or asked what it was or whether she could help. I skulked in my bedroom at the top of the house smoking and listening to Neil Young and Patti Smith. Sometimes I would sit at my desk, which Dad had made in woodwork class when he was at school, doing a little light work, but mainly I would play obsessive games of Patience, the small desk just large enough for the cards.

From time to time Mum would climb the stairs to my room when the music was so loud I hadn't heard the shout for supper, and wave away the clouds of smoke with her arms in a bad-tempered fashion, but that was about as disapproving as it got.

Both of them had a horror of pushy parenting. One evening an acquaintance of Mum's rang in a fever of anxiety over whether she should keep her daughter at South Hampstead, an academic private school, or move her to my school, where Mum also taught. The conversation went on, Mum rolling her eyes in exasperation, eventually saying it didn't matter very much as you could never know in advance where your child would flourish, so the only rational thing was to send them to the school that was closest.

The point of school, in her view, was that children should be happy, as only then would they be able to learn. I don't think she noticed that this theory was being disproved right under her nose by her middle child.

I was happy at school – or as happy as you can be in the thick of adolescence. I had good friends and it was fun sitting chatting to them in the smokers' common room, but I emerged from Camden with poor exam grades, eccentric spelling, and knowing nothing at all. The school offered a wonderful education to those girls who wanted to take it, but I didn't. Instead, what I acquired was a veneer of coolness and the idea that breaking rules was good if it made you seem different.

This was the 1970s, and progressives like my parents would have denied that education was about knowing things. They would have said it was more about skills, about learning how to think, and, most importantly, learning how to think originally. I would have accepted this myself until I started teaching. I now see that originality is a higher-order thing – it's not much use if you don't know the basics. Mum would have shuddered at the 'knowledge organisers' I give my pupils every few weeks, covering all the key facts that they must learn. But if I'd had a few of these myself, I might not have had to impose my lifelong ban on pub quizzes, which I avoid for fear of exposing my ignorance on practically every subject.

Looking back on it, my parents' laissez-faire approach was underpinned by two things, without which my education would have been a catastrophe. The first was belief – they both believed in me. They thought that I could do things, and because they thought that, so did I. Even now, 15 years after Mum's death and five years after Dad's, their belief in me makes me think I can become a good teacher. I can write this book. Why wouldn't I be able to?

The second was their own education. They were cultured Australians who had met at Oxford after the war. Our house was lined with books which they had not only read but had largely committed to memory. Both of them could – and did, at the drop of a hat – recite long chunks of Shakespeare over supper, correcting each other when they got stuck. Any shelves that were not packed with books housed Dad's collection of LPs, mainly Verdi and Schubert.

There have been many studies showing the biggest indicator of a child's success is how many books there are at home. The contents of our bookshelves were more obviously rubbing off on my literary sister Kate, who was reading English at Oxford, and on my musical brother Roland, who studied music at the Guildhall and wanted to be a professional oboist. The effects on me were – and still are – less noticeable: the only poem I can recite is the Blake one I've quoted above, which hardly counts given its excessively modest length, and I still prefer the Rolling Stones to Verdi. Yet the proximity to such culture had a big effect on me, even though I chose not to join in. I knew what highbrow looked like and it set a silent standard of what was expected of me.

There was another reason my parents shrugged off my A level results: they knew they weren't the important test.

Oxford had its own exams, which were less about memorising facts and more about spotting potential – and it was always silently assumed I'd sit them. I decided to apply for politics, philosophy and economics (PPE), mainly because I wasn't good enough at anything else. To get in I had to take two general papers, one in maths and one in English – which meant for the only time in my life I was taught by Mum.

She ran Oxbridge English classes at our house for all pupils in state schools in the Camden borough, putting the Formica tables together in our downstairs room to seat about 15 of us. Round that table was Emma Thompson, who went on to be an actor and all-round national treasure, but who was back then hard-working and oddly unconfident; Sean French, who became a journalist and novelist and was terrifyingly sure of his own opinions; and Lucy Heller, who went on to be my dearest friend and helped me set up Now Teach. I remember trying hard to say interesting things about Gerard Manley Hopkins – not, I think, because I wanted to impress Mum, but because I wanted to look clever in front of the others.

I can't have done very well in the exams as my first-choice college turned me down, but Lady Margaret Hall, where Mum had got a starred first, and where Kate had a scholarship and was also sailing her way towards a first, said it would interview me. The college had clearly thought: This latest Kellaway looks a dud on paper but maybe we should check, just to make sure.

The telegram arrived just before Christmas.

LADY MARGARET HALL OFFERS PLACE TO
READ PPE STOP CONGRATULATIONS STOP

On a minimum of work and with A level results that would have denied me access to any Russell Group university, I had got into one of the best universities in the world – in part thanks to the old-girl network. This stroke of good fortune changed my life. The Oxbridge badge did the magic thing it did for most of its graduates by opening doors to smart jobs, but an even bigger prize was the change inside my head. For eight hours a day, five days a week for three years, all I did was work. These were not the best years of my life; I was intermittently unhappier than I'd ever been before or since, but the only place I felt free from insecurities was in the library.

At first I worked to prove that I could and because I did not want ever again to be thought merely 'intuitive'. But as I sat there slogging, I found that I was actually interested in what I was studying, and came to have strong feelings for the marginal cost curve, propositional logic and Pareto optimisation.

My friend Lucy, who had got in to do the same course at the same college, had a room which looked out on mine, and she would see at all hours of the day her friend's hunched back bent over her desk. I wasn't the lazy girl she'd first met round our kitchen table trying hard to be cool. I'd transformed myself from idler to swot, an early reinvention that has dwarfed everything that's followed.

On a summer's day in 1981, wearing my black undergraduate gown, I went down to the Examination Schools on the High Street to read my results off a piece of paper on the wall. I scanned the short list of names of people who'd got first-class degrees. My name was not on it, but there it was, in the vast rump of seconds. This time the disappointment was sharp but brief. I'd got from Oxford what I wanted – I could pass as an academic person, I could spot the logical weakness in any argument, and I'd learnt how to work.

My life seemed set. I had a job lined up at J.P. Morgan in New York and an American boyfriend who was a PhD student, and I was about to go on holiday with him to Greece. Neither bank nor boyfriend would last – but I didn't know that then. What I did know was that the story of my formal education had ended well. By the skin of my teeth, I'd got away with it.

The moral of the story is this. I was born with all the cards stacked in my favour. I was a child of the 1970s where educational fashions were about teaching creativity rather than knowledge, which suited me fine, because I was from a highly educated family that, in the nicest possible way, expected big things from me. It is possible that the way Camden School for Girls taught me to break rules has helped me more in my career than my ignorance of the great river systems of the world has held me back. Either way, my new life in a Hackney comprehensive has made me see it from a different angle – the just-be-happy-darling school of education was a luxury for the middle classes – and even then it didn't always work.

January 2007

It is bollocking night at City of London, a private boys' school on the bank of the Thames, just below St Paul's Cathedral.

The school doesn't call it that. The letter in my handbag refers to a 'special, invitation-only parents' evening to discuss your son's performance', but I'm not deceived. Even though Arthur has only been at the school for a term, I know all is not well. I leave the *FT* office on the other side of the river slightly earlier than usual and, cursing slightly, hurry over the Millennium Bridge.

When Arty got a place at City of London, which educated Herbert Asquith, Kingsley Amis and, more recently, Daniel Radcliffe, I was jubilant. He'd been at a freewheeling state primary in Islington from which he'd emerged at the age of 11 able to read, though unwilling to do so, with some knowledge of basic maths and outlandish spelling and grammar. He had a halo of blond hair, badly cut by me into a longish pudding basin, and a remarkably sunny disposition.

The local secondary schools in Islington were dire in the early 2000s, and the result was an unseemly middle-class fight for places at North London's two selective state schools, and, for those able to scrape together the funds, at a few nearby private schools. The skirmish was everything that I had been brought up to despise, but there I was, in the middle of it.

On Saturday mornings I took Arty off to a tutor for whom he failed to do the set homework, and then proceeded to be turned down by most of the schools he'd applied to. But then, when all seemed lost, City of London offered him a place.

I don't remember that first term, except that Arty seemed cheerful enough in his black blazer with DOMINE DIRIGE NOS on the breast pocket. But the Lord didn't seem to be guiding him, and neither was his mother – nor his father, come to that, who was even more absent than I was, busy editing *Prospect*, the magazine he'd launched.

On that night in January, as I walked up the steps and into the hall where the bollocking was to be administered I noticed something odd. There were about 20 of us at this select gathering, women mostly unaccompanied by husbands or partners, each with the same harried look. All were white, professional working mothers. I recognised two of the others as mothers of Art's more gormless friends: one worked in TV, the other was a solicitor.

Each parent was paired up at a table with a teacher and sat down for a reprimand. I was told my son was doing badly in all subjects and what was needed was a system at home with strategies to ensure good working habits.

My 'system' was to come home from work, tired, to find he had done nothing. Here were some of the 'strategies' I deployed.

I tried to reason: if he did no work, he would get bad
grades and his life would be harder.
I tried to help, which ended up in shouting.
I bribed: If you do all your homework I'll let you play
Call of Duty.
I shouted more.
I went into denial, clinging to any sign that things
weren't too bad, and left him alone, hoping for the
best.
I confiscated Game Boys and laptops, hiding them in
ever more ingenious places which were invariably
discovered in a matter of hours.
Lowest of all, I used emotional blackmail. Sometimes
I would yell: 'I am working really hard giving speeches
to make extra money to pay for this school so that you
can do – NOTHING!'

In the end, his GCSEs were OKish, but thereafter things declined. At AS he did badly in everything but in economics he scored a U.

If the results were meant to be a wake-up call, Art remained fast asleep. One night during his mock A level exams I went downstairs to the basement in my nightdress at 3am to find him and his best friend drinking beer and playing pool on a broken table they had found in the street and carried home. I shouted at both of them, shaking with impotence and rage. Other things were unravelling by then. I was trying to look after Dad, who was lonely and getting increasingly feeble. My marriage was beginning its long slide towards ruin.

'Go to bed, Mum,' said Arty. 'You're out of control.'

By then Mum had been dead for seven years. I did not have her voice in my ear saying: Leave him alone – he'll be fine. David was more sanguine, but that may have been because he had long since outsourced homework to me and couldn't see how bad things were.

Through it I carried a bundle of guilt. Why were the children of some of my friends doing so much better than my son? One friend, who had given up her career when the first of her four children were born, had read them Greek fables from the age of two and denied them computers until they were in their teens. I watched all four glide from one academic triumph to the next with a sour taste in my mouth.

Had something gone wrong for the sons of families with two working parents, whose parenting style oscillated between laissez-faire and competitive hysteria? I think back to the bollocking night and contrast it to the prizegiving ceremony that took place later that same term. This involved spending two hours clapping other people's children and I was profoundly bored – until I noticed a pattern.

City is a multicultural school and nearly all maths and science prizes were won by Chinese boys, apart from a few which were won by kids from the Indian subcontinent. After them came the Jewish kids, who scooped up most of the humanities and debating prizes. Bringing up the rear was the class of which my son was a member, rich gentiles paying full school fees. Towards the end a kid called Oscar with long blond curls won a prize for his artwork, but that was about it.

Back then, when I didn't know what a hard time of it we'd be in for, I watched with some satisfaction. The boys from immigrant families did far better because they worked harder – and I hoped some of that would rub off on my son.

What happened was the reverse. Arty later explained that these boys were so very much better than him, there was no point in competing; the only sensible thing to do was to play computer games instead. I thought bitterly of the advantage kids are supposed to have being in houses with books in them. There were so many books in David's study the ceiling below was in danger of collapsing, but still Arty read nothing.

He says his refusal to work was also because he was too happy. He didn't believe any of my warnings that he was ruining his life chances. His existence seemed so comfortable it was impossible for his adolescent brain to imagine that it might stop being so.

On A levels results day, he went to school to get his results while I sat staring at my phone. The only message I got that morning was from a mother with a son in the same year:

Joe got two A*s and an A. Relief! Hope news good your end??

By lunchtime the message came:

I'll pay you back the money I owe you.

I read this and cried. Not because it meant he'd done even worse than expected, but out of shame. How could I have made him feel guilty about the cost of private school, when the decision to send him there was mine?

That autumn, Art got a job in Hot Wok, a Chinese take-away in the next street from our house. This might not have seemed like a great first step on the ladder but it was where his education began. Within a month he had acquired more motivation than in seven years at one of the country's finest private schools. He'd made friends with some of the chefs, who were on minimum wage and were failing to support their families. He decided then that he had better get some qualifications after all.

Meanwhile, I'd been doing some research and found that he could go to Nottingham to do engineering with his Cs in maths and physics so long as he did a foundation year. We visited, he applied, he duly got a place.

Just as I'd done before him, Art buckled down and stayed buckled down, emerging five years later with a first-class MEng in electrical and electronic engineering. His reasoning was the same as mine: he worked because he hated wearing the badge of academic failure. He'd also given himself a monumental fright and was not going to let that happen again.

The moral of his story is similar to mine. He got away with it, partly because he had middle-class parents who found a way. He could afford to fail, because he had a safety net.

I have just shown him what I've written. He doesn't mind being portrayed as a wastrel, because he is one no longer. He has a job as a data scientist in a start-up and is motivated and doing well.

But what about all the shouting and nagging? Did it make a difference? Art now says it was counterproductive – as well as being unpleasant – anything resembling coercion automatically makes him inclined to do the reverse. Has he forgiven me for it? He says he has, but I'm not entirely sure I've forgiven myself.

January 2020

I am sitting in the school sports hall behind a small table with a bottle of water on it and a piece of paper displaying a list of students' names together with their predicted grades. On the other side of the table is Khalid, a 15-year-old hulk, and Khalid's mum, who looks about 20 and is wearing a headscarf.

> Me: Khalid's natural grasp of economics is good and I
> think he enjoys the subject – don't you, Khalid?
> Khalid: Yes, Miss.
> Me: But he only got a 2 in his mock and he really has to
> do some more work.

I am in the middle of a three-hour Year 11 parents' evening. This ought to be hell, as it comes at the end of a full-on day of teaching, but I am thoroughly enjoying myself. Finally, the boot is on the other foot. For each of my own four children I spent 14 years sitting where Khalid's mum is now, at the mercy of their teachers. Now it's my turn.

The trouble is, I'm not sure about the right line to take. Everything I thought I knew about learning and motivation based on my own education and Arty's does not apply. At this school, working hard is compulsory. There is no nonsense about happiness or creativity – this is about getting exam results. If the pupils don't work, they get punished, and if the parents fail to turn up to parents' evening, they get told off too.

The next pupil to come to my desk is Jade, a sweet, hardworking girl who is on free school meals and is also the weakest in the class. She turns up with a silent mother and four younger siblings in tow, two of whom climb onto her lap. I tell the mother that her daughter's work ethic is phenomenal. I say I know she sometimes finds the subject hard (massive understatement) but that she really deserves to pass. Jade is a wonderful person, I say, and I hope that her mother feels very proud indeed. The whole family beams – even the little kids.

I sometimes wonder if Arty had been to this school whether he might have picked up Jade's work ethic. If he had been forced by the school to work, would he have tried more? I suspect he would have been more like my next customer, Zian, who is approaching my table now.

Or rather, Zian's mother is approaching. Zian himself has not deigned to show up, on the grounds, she tells me, that he's poorly. This boy is a problem: he is funny and loveable but he never works if he can avoid it. His beleaguered mother reminds me of myself, only that she is barely half my age, is wearing a headscarf and is very pretty. She says she has tried everything with him, but to no avail. I tell her I've given him multiple pep talks and so many detentions for undone or sloppy work that I'm running out of options. We wring our hands together, which is therapeutic, if not terribly helpful.

In Zian I see Arty, only there is one big difference between the two idlers. Arty had a safety net under him. Zian does not.

In four months' time these kids will sit their GCSEs and the stakes could not be higher. If they do well they will leave this school, which has no Sixth Form, bound for somewhere decent to sit their A levels. A few will go on to great universities and the world in all its gloriousness will beckon. If they do badly, they will go to a college that admits teenagers who have already failed, with a high chance that they will be spat out two years later with no qualifications and the prospect of a life of delivering pizza from the back of a bicycle. There are few second chances.

To try to get them over the line, I want to understand which works better on an evening like this: stick or carrot? My school is big on sticks and while I'm coming around to them a bit, I'm still sufficiently scarred by my experience with Arty and indoctrinated by my own upbringing to think there might be something in a carrot. In any case, my recent experience at previous parents' evenings has made me think twice before giving the parents of lazy kids too much of a beating.

In my first year, when I was a trainee maths teacher, I told the father of one boy who was both sneaky and lazy that his work ethic was deplorable and he would certainly fail unless he changed his approach entirely. The parent scowled. The child scowled. He already disliked maths – and me. After that he liked it and me even less.

What really put me off telling parents the unvarnished truth was a Year 9 student called Daniel. He was often in trouble, did his homework in five minutes, and was mainly interested in goading his Ghanaian friend by saying his

Nigerian jollof rice was better than anything produced in Ghana. I had planned to have a sharp word with his parents, but then I spotted them getting up from a meeting with one of the science teachers. The mother's face was set in a mask of rage and Daniel was crying. My yelling at Arty suddenly seemed tame by comparison to this West African version of heavy parenting. When the pair sat down at my table I told the incandescent mother that her son was a fine young man and a pleasure to have in my class. His homework, I said, was not quite as thorough as some of the other students, but I was sure that would come as he matured. The result: Daniel was still lazy and his work did not improve noticeably, but I think he liked business studies – and me – more than before. I don't teach him anymore but he shouts, 'Hello, Miss Kellaway!' whenever he sees me in the playground.

To do my job better I need to understand the answer to a more fundamental question than sticks or carrots: why does one child work and the other doesn't? Why is Jade a Stakhanovite and Zian a lotus-eater? There are a few universal truths: girls work harder than boys, I suspect mainly because they are less complacent. There is also a work ethic built into the fabric of some families, particularly some of the immigrant ones, that strikes me as both wonderful and entirely alien.

But I still want to know what it is exactly that makes students work hard. So one day at school I decided to ask them myself. I constructed a list of all the things I could think of that might make them spend longer on their homework, and wrote them on a slide for the class to see.

1. To avoid detentions/getting into trouble
2. To please your parents
3. Because you love the subject
4. To impress your teachers
5. To get good exam results, and go to a good university
6. Because it will lead to a good job and more money
7. To do better than your friends

Because the school is run on fear I suspected the biggest lever would be detentions, which are freely dispensed to anyone whose work is not up to scratch. This turned out only to be true of my most disengaged students, and even then fear came from home rather than school. 'I work or I get yelled at by parents,' one of them explained. Instead, the biggest motivator turned out to be one that would not have occurred to me or to my son in a million years – money. My students spend more time on their homework today because they believe it will one day make them rich – or stop them from being poor.

'I work so I can provide for my family when I'm grown up,' one student wrote. Others said: 'So I can have a big house'; 'I wanna earn loadz of money', and, most tragically: 'I don't want to be homeless in the future.'

Hardly anyone said that impressing their teachers mattered (which was a slight downer), and no one said they spent more time on their homework because they found it interesting. I look at the results and feel sad that the kids think intellectual effort is only worthwhile if it might lead to money one day – but then I feel ashamed of my response. The reason it never occurred to me as a teenager that there was a link between effort and future riches was because my parents never suggested as much. When they emigrated from Australia in the 1940s they were escaping not poverty but the cultural desert that Melbourne was back then. They were never poor, so the chances of my becoming so were minuscule.

Two middle-class students gave answers that stood out from the rest. One girl, who I spotted reading Zadie Smith's *White Teeth* when she was just 12, wrote: 'I strive to be successful so I can do what I enjoy when I'm older.' A boy who swaggers his way around school as if to broadcast his feeling of superiority said he was motivated by none of my options. 'I work because I wan't [sic] to change the world.'

The survey, asked of 25 students, wasn't scientific. Neither was it objective, as they may have been giving the answers that they felt were expected of them.

Yet even so, the scanty results were a reminder that many of the children I teach are from poor families, which is clearly going to give them a different idea of the imperative of making money than the richer ones.

But what does this mean for the strength of their motivation? Does the child who wants to change the world work harder or better than the one who doesn't want to be poor? Not according to my sample. The former, who is from a middle-class background, is a dilettante. He expends a little effort when he feels inclined, but usually doesn't bother. In fact, he is so lazy that despite his considerable intelligence he managed to get an elementary mistake into his single sentence. The boy who wants to provide for his future family slogs his guts out – the neat, well-written answers he handed in to me were typical of all his work.

My last student of the evening comes to sit down. She is an Eastern European girl who is both clever and exceptionally hard-working. I tell her mother that she should aim for one of the country's best universities and that I hope she'll study economics.

Mihaela: What university did you go to, Miss?
Me: Oxford.
Mihaela: Wow! Did you work really hard to get in?
Me: Um … you work even harder.

Which is the understatement of the century.

10

Re-Education

The picture was taken on a sunny day in 1968 in the playground at Gospel Oak Primary School in North London. I am sitting cross-legged in the front row, wearing a pink-and-orange flowery mini-dress and new hippy sandals that were made by my friend Tabitha's mum. There are 34 of us: 17 boys and 17 girls. We are third-year juniors, which means we are all either nine or ten and, with the exception of the girl sitting a few along from me, we are all white. She had one Asian parent, which made her so outlandish I can still remember her more than half a century later.

I have just unfurled a long school photo taken on the netball court of Camden School for Girls in 1976. I'm at the back as I'm by now in the Sixth Form. This time I've got a pageboy haircut and am wearing a purple poloneck that came from Biba, the mecca of fashion on Kensington High Street. Even though there is no school uniform we all look much the same: 700 almost exclusively white girls in mainly cheesecloth and jumbo-flares, from predominantly middle-class intellectual(ish) Labour-voting families.

Though my childhood was white, it was not quite as white as those of my Australian parents. Mum had never seen anyone Black until she came to England on holiday when she was nine, and reported being profoundly shocked. Dad did not want us to grow up like that, and when I was about eight a Nigerian family rented the flat in our basement. We were friendly enough, but we never really got to know them – all I really remember are the pretty bows in their baby's hair and the unfamiliar smell of their cooking.

After school I went to Lady Margaret Hall, Oxford. Here it was the same story, only posher. After some digging, I've found the matriculation picture. There I am, wearing my black sub fusc hat at a ridiculously rakish angle and pouting babyishly at the camera. I think I'm trying to prove I'm different from this mainly privately educated group of young women. I had no idea what to make of the Hon. Libby Manners, who was rumoured to be going out with Prince Charles. Or of Domenica Fraser, who later surprised me by inviting me to her wedding, and then surprised (and thrilled) me further when one of the other guests turned out to be Princess Diana. Throughout my time at Oxford I played the inverted snob: I constantly reminded myself and anyone else who showed any interest that I'd gone to a state grammar school and wasn't at all posh, since my parents were Australians who were a schoolteacher and a librarian. This now strikes me as pathetic: I was merely splitting hairs.

There is no group photo of my year at J.P. Morgan, the investment bank I joined after leaving Oxford, but I don't need one as I remember the line-up well enough. On my training programme there were nine of us: all Oxbridge, all white. I was the 'diversity hire' not due to my race or class, but because I was the only woman. When I joined the *Financial Times* two years later, it was the same thing all over again. Journalism was ever so slightly more female than banking but back then it was no more racially mixed.

By the time I was 58 I had spent the best part of six decades associating exclusively with people who were just like me only more so. My friends were mainly Oxbridge, almost all middle-class, and all white save two or three. I sometimes felt sheepish about such narrowness, but never thought it was my fault. I was merely a product of class, generation, education and profession: it couldn't be helped.

Neither did I think my world was narrow. My friends may have been socially and ethnically peas in a pod, but their views seemed delightfully various. Most journalists are good at arguing – and no one liked it better than the one I'd married, who was so skilled at disagreeing with almost anyone on almost anything that in 2019 he was shortlisted for the Contrarian Prize.

I remember one evening around 2009 going to dinner with neighbours in Highbury and finding myself sitting next to Jon Snow. This was hugely pleasing, as I'd been admiring his coloured socks (as had Mum) on telly since 1989 when he started presenting *Channel Four News*. What was less pleasing was that over pudding he and David had an argument so nasty it stopped every conversation around the table and ended the evening. Both men were scarlet-faced, yelling and jabbing their forefingers at each other. Had the table not been so wide, I daresay one of them would have hit the other. I think Jon took the view that it was a disgrace that more guilty bankers had not been locked up for causing the financial crisis. I can't remember David's line so rang him just now to ask.

> Me: Do you remember having that row with Jon Snow
> at Kate and Charles's house about locking up bankers?
> David (*laughs*): Yes.
> Me: What was your argument?
> David: No idea. I hope I stood up for bankers.

Never did it occur to me that under the roar of this and many other arguments, everyone in my remit thought more or less the same things. I lived in a bubble which from the inside seemed stimulating and capacious, but which now strikes me as tiny.

Very slowly the penny is dropping: at work now I'm in a wide world where I am in a minority on almost everything: class, outlook, income, age, hair colour and, most obviously, ethnicity. The people I meet have different views to mine, as a result of their very different experiences of life so far. In this new world I'm an innocent and a know-nothing who is stumbling about clumsily. To survive I'm having to make a complete breach with my old columnist way of thinking, according to which, if I had a view on something and if the last two people I'd spoken to had the same view then it must be a) right and b) what every sensible person in the world must think too.

Now I teach in a school where my pupils' families are from all over the world: first-, second- and sometimes third-generation immigrants from Nigeria and Ghana, from the Caribbean, form Turkey and Bangladesh and Vietnam. Most of my classes have a small handful of white students in them, and many of them come from Eastern Europe and elsewhere.

My ignorance of these communities was shamefully obvious from the first time I set foot in a classroom and was expected to take a register. There were 32 names on the computer screen in front of me, of which only ten I could pronounce without effort. I could just about do Yusuf. But what about Kujoe, Igbekoyi or Djimon? Tariq I thought I was fine with, thanks to Tariq Ali. I confidently pronounced it 'Tar-reek', but the little boy under my nose corrected me. It was 'Tah-rik'. I am feeble with names anyway, and when I come upon long ones written down I never pronounce them in my head, but note the first letter and scan the general shape. There is no such let-out when you have a live class in front of you. Name after name I mispronounced. I felt I had a large sign over my head that read: THIS WOMAN IS A COMPLETE IDIOT. SHE IS ALMOST CERTAINLY A RACIST TOO.

I got better quickly because I had to, and now the names are so familiar I can't remember why they ever seemed so hard. But I've gone on making other, worse, mistakes. In my second year I was teaching a business studies class about ethics. I had shown the class an advertisement for Gillette which was causing a hoo-ha on social networks because the brand had taken it upon itself to give all men a lesson on how not to pinch women's bottoms and behave obnoxiously. The result was mass offence from Gillette's loyal customers, some of whom filmed themselves throwing away their razors.

Student: Miss, why did Gillette do that?
Me: Companies are desperate to prove to the world that they are whiter than white.

There was an intake of breath. The old-fashioned phrase, which had seemed so innocuous as it formed in my head, was ugly and wrong the minute it emerged from my mouth into the classroom. The atmosphere in the room was tense. A couple of the students exchanged glances as if to say: 'What the hell?! Did she really say that?!'

In the next split second I made a calculation. Should I stop the lesson and apologise? Should I acknowledge that some of them were offended, and explain that 'whiter than white' came from a Persil advertisement from the 1970s, and for me had no racial subtext? Or might this open an entire Pandora's box of grievances? I decided to plough on and pretend nothing had happened. Because the school is so strict and the students so cowed no one challenged me directly, but I was shaken. It is a phrase I will never use again.

This, alas, was not an isolated incident. Until I started teaching I would often say so-and-so had a 'black mark' against their name. It had never occurred to me that there was anything the matter with this, until one day the phrase fell out of my mouth in class. I looked at the expressions on the two Black faces in the front row. I then saw there was much wrong with it. This phrase I have also put in the bin.

That evening an old journalist friend came to dinner and I told him about my assorted gaffes, and explained that I had had to spring-clean my entire cupboard of phrases to make sure that none of them sounded racist.

'How ridiculous!' he exclaimed. '"Black mark" isn't racist, it's part of the language! And you aren't racist in using it. I'm amazed that you, of all people, who used to be the most fearlessly un-PC person I know, are giving in to all this.'

There had been no 'giving in', I snapped. It wasn't a question of being 'politically correct'. The matter was as simple as this: if I say something that causes offence to my students then I have to learn to stop saying it. Right away. More than that, if I were to go on using a phrase that I knew caused offence, that would be blatantly racist – as well as entirely boneheaded.

My antediluvian clangers have rattled me and have raised a question I don't know the answer to. When I am teaching, is it my job to think about race all the time, or not at all? I had thought the latter: it is my job to teach teenagers that a positive externality is a wondrous thing. If I make a good fist of this I'm helping them: it's as simple as that. I have a duty to teach the Bangladeshi boy who shares a two-room flat with his mother and five siblings, just as I have a duty to teach the white girl who lives in a big house on Victoria Park and whose father in a high-up exec at the BBC. That was what I used to think. Now I'm not so sure.

A couple of months into my first year as a trainee teacher, I volunteered to help with the after-school debating club. I thought I'd be in my element: I might not yet have figured out how to teach, but I do know how to argue. The club was run by an inspirational young English teacher who liked nothing better than an incendiary motion. One day he picked 'This house believes there should be quotas for ethnic-minority teachers' – a particularly sensitive topic given that in this school non-white students made up 70 per cent of the total, while the overwhelming majority of the teachers, particularly the senior ones, were white.

It was my job to coach the team on the side of the proposition, but they needed no help from me in coming up with three supporting arguments.

1. Black teachers are better role models to Black students. Students respect teachers, and it is important to see people of the same race doing jobs that teenagers look up to.
2. Black students are more comfortable seeking help and advice from Black teachers who are more likely to understand some of their problems.
3. The only way of getting more Black teachers is through quotas; otherwise they are held back by racism.

I sat on the plastic school chair feeling increasingly uncomfortable. The debate, won by a mile by my side, didn't make me feel apologetic for being white but it did make me wonder whether I could be quite as useful as a teacher in this school as I hoped I would be.

Soon after this, my school was looking for a new business studies teacher, and I found myself sitting at the back of my classroom as the hopefuls showed what they could do, live in front of my students. One of the candidates was a Black man of almost my age with a heavy West African accent. Before he had even put his memory stick into my computer to load the first slide I noticed something odd. Two of my students who usually sit through my lessons in a sulk just mild enough to avoid a detention underwent an astonishing transformation. Ekon, my most unresponsive student, had his hand up wanting to help the teacher with the computer. After the lesson Amare came up to me in the playground, face shining with enthusiasm, and asked if the teacher would be teaching him next year. I was hurt and confounded.

Back in the maths office, I relayed the incident to my mentor, Marcel. He shrugged and said there would always be a few Black kids who would show their preference for being taught by a Black teacher, but that the best way to get their respect was to do what I was doing – to show you care and to know your subject inside out.

This was a typically sweet response from Marcel, who was born in Hackney to parents from the Caribbean and was much loved by all students (and by me). But I didn't feel entirely reassured.

When I first started teaching at this school, I never brought up race with Marcel or the man who became my other great friend in the department, Kwame, who had moved from Ghana to London a decade earlier to become a teacher. We politely ignored our differences and discussed what we had in common: the kids, the school, teaching. But as I got to know them better, race was the subject I most wanted to discuss. I wanted to hear their experiences. And I needed some help to understand my own. Both of them would sometimes tell me about subtle and not so subtle discrimination that Black teachers sometimes face in London schools. As I have never been on the receiving end of racism I have tended to downplay other people's accounts of it. But I listened to their accounts of teachers getting passed over for promotion and put down and ignored. Marcel assured me, in the nicest possible way, that I would never quite get it but it was good, he said, that I was trying to.

One day I saw Kwame in the playground surrounded by a group of Black boys. What was that about, I asked him later? He said he was often sought out by pupils who felt they were being given a hard time, their customary complaint being that they got more detentions than the white students. This was something I'd noticed too – when it is my turn to run after-school detentions for my department I have once or twice found myself in the uncomfortable position of being the sole white person in the room sitting at the teacher's desk and meting out punishment to a room full of Black students, mainly boys.

If I do an audit of the detentions I hand out myself, it is true that a disproportionate number are to Black boys. In each case I'm pretty sure they deserved the punishment, having broken one of the school's many rules. But what I'm not so sure about is whether there are other students (who might be white or might be girls) I've let off the hook. This is another thing to worry about.

The more I think about it, the more I'm sure I'm a bundle of unconscious biases. I know my heart is in the right place on race, but my heart is an unreliable organ when it comes to crossing this particular minefield.

Before I started teaching I didn't think much about racism. I told myself that things had got a lot better in the UK during my lifetime and I assumed they'd continue to improve. The answer was to provide good education to every student and then all races would live happily ever after.

That was before the murder of George Floyd. It was also before I judged a public speaking competition open to all secondary schools in Hackney. Every school entered two 15-year-olds who each gave a speech on any topic they wanted to talk about.

On the night I sat on the judges' table in an assembly hall and listed to two dozen teenagers do something that I hadn't known how to do when I was in my 40s, project my voice and speak from the heart, without notes. Of the finalists, eight were Black girls, the first of whom gave a powerful and heart-felt talk about how she, as a Black woman, felt marginalised. The next girl gave a talk about how ideals of female beauty did not include Black beauty. Six further talks followed along similar lines. The performances varied from medium to electrifying, but the topics were broadly the same. All of the eight talked about feeling in one way or another disadvantaged by being young, Black and female.

The judging took place about 100 yards from where I live. But I might as well have stepped into another world. Why was this the only thing they all wished to talk about? Why wasn't there a single Black girl who felt moved to discuss the sorts of things the white students talked about: plastic in the sea, losing a mother to cancer, or the dangerous power wielded by Amazon?

Listening to the speeches I saw that for these students it is irrelevant whether there is less racism than there used to be. When I come across sexism now, I don't think: It's no big deal because in the past women didn't have the vote. The issue is what is happening now, and these students' perception of that is alarming.

I don't know what the answer is in policy terms. I don't even know what – if anything – I can do about it in my own classroom. In the absence of any better ideas, all I can do for now is to ask my students questions, to listen to them when they tell me about their world, and tell them about mine. I am educating them and they are educating me.

I'm leaning over the shoulder of a 12-year-old student, looking at her exercise book. I've asked the class to order $\frac{1}{6}$, $\frac{1}{2}$ and $\frac{1}{3}$ by size starting with the biggest, and in her neat, round script Hayley has written: $\frac{1}{6}$, $\frac{1}{3}$, $\frac{1}{2}$. I look at the work of the boy sitting behind her who has given the same answer, only his writing is so bad you might have thought he'd written it with his foot. Most of the class seems to agree: one-sixth is the biggest fraction.

This is especially disappointing as I've just spent ten minutes drawing pizzas on the board and dividing them into different numbers of slices. Faced with the pizzas, they could see that a half was the biggest piece – but once the pizzas are gone they don't have a clue.

Nothing in my life prepared me for this. From the time I got into Camden grammar school I was cut off from 75 per cent of society by dint of having passed some tests. Going to Oxford represented a further narrowing, and a further one after that when I got a job at the *FT.* For 30 years I worked in an environment where academic success was so much the norm it was easy to forget anything else existed.

But there I was, in my first month as a trainee teacher, surrounded by children who seemed unable to do things I would have thought too obvious to need any explanation. In my school 40 out of 180 students in Year 7 were in bottom sets, and all of them had difficulty grasping anything that was ever so slightly abstract.

At some point in that first term I went to a training session on growth mindsets – the idea that anyone can get better at anything with a bit of hard work and encouragement. It was led by a priggish young teacher who gave us a lecture on the importance of having high expectations of all students. I pointed out that the problem with my Year 7s wasn't that my expectations were awry but that their ability level was so low and I was so inexperienced that my inept explanations were not getting through.

'Can I suggest,' she said in a sugary voice with head held to one side, 'that you be careful about using the term "low-ability"?'

My vocabulary could be interpreted, she warned, as evidence that I didn't have the right growth mindset myself. The correct term was 'low prior attainment' – which suggested that poor attainment would shortly be a thing of the past. What total PC bollocks, I thought to myself. Whose interests were served by this soppy pretence that everyone is equally able, when this was so evidently not the case?

Now I'm not so sure. Even though 'low prior attainment' doesn't trip off the tongue, the more time I spend with teenagers the more I see the problem with attaching an ability label to them.

Every December and June my school gym fills with Year 11 students sitting exams. To the left of the room the top set files in, after them the middle sets, and finally the bottom set, who sit on the right by the fire exit. Whenever I invigilate I walk up and down the ranks of students and each time I am struck by something uncomfortable. The children on the left are predominantly white and middle-class. The ones on the right are mainly Black students with a sprinkling of white working-class ones thrown in for good measure, and most are pupil premium, which means they are from poor families. On the left, heads are bent over desks and hands wave in the air asking for more paper. On the right many students stop writing halfway through and spend the rest of the time staring unhappily into space. The first time I saw this I thought: OK, I get it. To say that the kids on the left are clever and the ones on the right are not isn't correct. It is more complicated – and more unfair – than that. Some have been born lucky, others less so. The school, and every teacher in it, busts a gut to redress the balance, but it's not easy.

Now that I've spent longer teaching there is another reason I try not to put ability labels on students: the word is too narrow. Last year I had a student called Desiree who, no matter how hard I tried to explain it, could not comprehend that the demand curve slopes downwards. One day I decided to stage a fake World Economic Forum press conference at Davos, and got my class to play Prince Charles, Donald Trump and Greta Thunberg. With some misgivings I gave Desiree the part of Trump, and found that although the simplest academic tasks defeated her, being President of the United States was well within her reach. Desiree electrified the class with a Trump-like contortion of her bottom lip and the way she pointed and shouted 'Fake news!' and 'Make America great again!'

To do that this 14-year-old had to be able to watch Trump closely, pay attention to every nuance, and then copy it sensitively, with bits added for humour – all of which takes more skill and is arguably more useful than being able to identify a demand curve. But where is our respect and appreciation for that?

The other day I was discussing this with David, who has just written a book called *Head Hand Heart*, in which he argues that we overvalue academic achievements and underrate everything else. I have spent much of my life disagreeing with him politically, but on the undervaluing of Desiree, we are shoulder to shoulder.

He says schools should help children like her by placing a higher value on music, drama and sport and making everyone do practical subjects alongside academic ones. When I was at school, he says, we all had to do woodwork. I don't point out that one would never have guessed this from his current DIY skills, but instead say he may be partly right.

David talks with all the confidence of the armchair theorist, but I'm encumbered with knowledge of real children and so see it as far more complicated. Maybe schools should teach more practical subjects and maybe we should value drama differently. But that's not the world I'm in. My problem is more mundane: how do I help the students who struggle academically right now?

Teachers change lives. I don't know how many times I've heard this trite phrase since entering the profession but every time I do I wince. My collection of lives changed so far can be counted on one finger, and that student was not one from the right of the gym whose life was most in need of change, but was a bright but lazy boy in Year 9. One day in class I mentioned in passing how much investment bankers earned and at the end of the lesson Jaward stayed behind to ask how he could become one. I told him that although I could see him as a successful banker, he didn't have a hope unless he got top grades – and he had no hope of getting those unless he started working right now. The transformation was instant and lasting. This boy is no longer slightly below the middle of my class but is one of my top two performers. Maybe when the history books are written on Jaward, the visionary financier, I will have played a bit part in changing his life because I accidentally planted a seed and then tried to water it. Even though I didn't go into teaching to swell the bloated ranks of investment bankers, the day Jaward gets a job at Goldman Sachs I will dance a jig.

Yet I absolutely failed to change the lives of Jordan and Deniz, two boys from the bottom set who I taught for business studies in my first year at the school and who both left without managing even the lowest pass grade I had predicted for them. I recently ran into the pair lurking in the churchyard close to my house, sitting on the tomb of someone who'd died 300 years earlier, drumming their heels into the side of it.

Mostly I like bumping into my students outside school. I enjoy rounding the corner from the tinned goods aisle in Sainsbury's and finding myself staring at Destiny from Year 9. I loved running into Demarcus from Year 10 one Saturday night as I was dashing to catch a train, and didn't recognise the cool dude in his trainers and puffa jacket until he approached to give me a spontaneous and entirely surprising hug. But I wasn't altogether pleased to see these two 16-year-olds.

Jordan: Hello, Miss!
Me: How are you, Jordan? Hello, Deniz.

Jordan: Good, Miss, good.

Me: How's college?

Jordan: S'right.

Me: Why aren't you there now?

Jordan: Don't need to be, Miss. It's pretty chilled.

I taught these students for a year and left no mark on their lives. I failed to get either of them to understand the basics of cash flow or of marketing matrices. I didn't know how to begin.

Two years later, I have a clearer idea of what it is I'm trying to do. Changing lives turns out not to be about making instant transformations – it is about hard slog and tiny, incremental improvements. This realisation has changed my own life – or at least how I teach, and the sort of teacher I want to be.

Before I started teaching I thought the best teachers were the ones who were incapable of dullness and who could inspire their students to think big. I was determined that my lessons would be an entertaining spectacle with me going at full throttle, a cross between Miss Jean Brodie, Hector from *The History Boys* and my mum. I saw myself leading my students out into the big, wide world and making them love GDP as much as Mum made hers love Gerard Manley Hopkins.

To my delight, the first time I stood up in a classroom to teach economics I found being this flamboyant teacher was easy. Rogue comes naturally if you have spent your whole life writing sarky newspaper columns.

Back then, I went through the motions of teaching the curriculum – straying at the smallest excuse. One day when I was meant to be teaching the labour market I spent half the lesson demonstrating to the class the correct way to ask for a pay rise. Just as I had got them all to role-play tight-fisted bosses and aggrieved employees, a senior member of staff walked into my classroom and afterwards asked me what I was doing. I explained that while this wasn't exactly on the curriculum it was something good to know: if only someone had taught me this when I was 15 I wouldn't have had to wait until I was nearly 50 to try it out. She laughed and let it go.

One day I went off on a long, impassioned rant about how modern economists are questioning whether budget deficits matter. The discussion pinged to and fro between my six economics stars, and I was just congratulating myself on the quality of the lesson when Alicia, who had sat through it in her customary silence, stayed behind to talk to me. She said she didn't understand what we were talking about, but as I started to explain budget deficits to her she stopped me. She told me she didn't understand anything in economics. She said she was doing worse in it than in any of her other subjects – and then she started to cry. As the enormity of this landed I felt like crying myself.

Sometimes I wonder how Miss Jean Brodie or my mum would have fared with students like Alicia. Their pupils mostly found learning easy and just needed to be pointed in the right direction, whereas Alicia needed actual, skilful teaching of a sort I simply was not providing. In my more spiteful moments I fancied both of them would have been making an even worse fist of it than I was.

Since that day the penny has dropped: the best way of helping Alicia is not to try to make economics a fun show, it is to get her to pass her exam. If it is a teacher's job to open doors, those doors, under the present regime, are GCSEs.

When I started teaching, I thought exams were a necessary evil. I still think that. I hate the way schools talk of them as if they are the purpose of education, when in fact they are merely (flawed) evidence that you've acquired some. I despised the government's response to Covid in schools, where it prioritised the year groups taking exams, as if the education of the other years somehow didn't matter. I despair at the way teachers spend as much time teaching exam technique as the subject itself. Yet despite this I, too, am teaching the exam first and economics second.

What I must do became even clearer to me after the first lockdown, during which 50 per cent of my students – and 100 per cent of those who were already struggling – took a five-month sabbatical from learning anything at all. When they returned to school in September all my idealistic notions about trying to acquaint them with the world in general were forced out the window – exams were bearing down and the world was going to have to wait.

On the first day back, I started easy. What is GDP, I asked the class? We had spent six whole weeks studying this before lockdown and so I thought this was a safe question to put to one of my most vulnerable students. He looked at me through a fog of uncertainty. 'General … demand … production?' he offered. This boy was eight months away from sitting his economics GCSE. He needed to pass; it was my job to help him.

One day last November in the grim era when students sat through lessons wearing face masks and when I started each class by squirting pink disinfectant on every desk, the deputy head put his head round my door. He caught me at the whiteboard modelling a perfect six-mark question on the board while the students copied it down. Afterwards I explained to him that the maverick was dead.

When I decided to be a teacher, there were two things in my mind. I suspected (rightly) that I would love showing off at the front of the class. I also suspected (rightly) that I would get pleasure from being useful.

What has changed is my understanding that the two are linked. I've discovered there is little fun in showing off for the sake of it; it only feels good if you know you are being useful too. One day, when I'm more experienced, I still hope I may be able to do both – to be rogue and exam stickler at the same time. But for now, for all my students but especially for those who struggle most, I know the sort of teacher I need to become. My prior attainment in this area is indisputably low, but I'm aiming to be the greatest exam stickler the world has ever seen.

11

Young-Old

June 2019, Hackney

I am lying on the sofa at home in a black lace party dress. Two of Stan's friends are ripping open cartons of beer and Prosecco and putting the bottles into bins filled with ice. A young cook and her boyfriend have taken charge of the orange worktop and are making industrial quantities of potato salad in washing-up basins.

It is my 60th birthday party and this time it's going to be different. I am paying other people to do the work for me and, even more radically, have decided not to worry. Every party I've ever given has been ruined by anxiety, and even though right now I can see that there isn't nearly enough food for the hundred or so people who said they'd come, I am forcing myself not to care. It's my party and far from crying if I want to, I'm hell-bent on having the best possible time. I tell myself if anyone is hungry they can get a takeaway on the way home.

I think back to my 50th party, ten years ago yesterday, held in the garden at Highbury. My marriage was failing and the celebration felt like a sham. I remember being jumped into giving an impromptu speech and found myself holding forth about Michael Jackson, singer and child molester, whom I claimed was almost my twin since he'd died the day before. It was neither funny nor birthday-ish.

Today, the party is going to be the same but different. I am in the same dress for continuity, which is backless and which I've had to adapt by sewing on some dark T-shirt material to reduce the extent of aging flesh it reveals. All four children are the same but different, a decade older and all with their own lives, which they have interrupted to celebrate with me. Rose arrived this morning from Ghana, where she is teaching, and surprised me as I was standing at the counter making myself coffee. Stan has come home early from a surfing holiday. Maud has travelled the shorter distance from Brixton, and Arty, who is living with me, has spent the day writing a speech in which he will tell everyone that my new vocation was not apparent earlier in life from the way I used to scream at him over his maths homework. David has come all the way from his Hampstead flat, bearing his usual heavy bag of reading material, which I've made him stow under the stairs.

I ask one of Stan's friends to take a photo before the guests come. The six of us sit on a bench in the garden – the same one we sat on for a picture 20 years earlier – but this time we don't all fit on – David, Maud and I are seated – a bit precariously as the slats are now partly rotten and are held together with gaffer tape – while Arty and Rosie perch on the arms. Stan, who was on my knee 20 years ago, now has a beard and is sprawled on the ground, emaciated as he's picked up a stomach bug on holiday. Later I show the picture to a friend who says: 'This is your greatest achievement.' She's wrong – my children aren't my achievement. They are their own agents, trying to navigate their lives with intermittent and inconsistent interference from me. I don't even see it as an achievement that David and I are somehow friends. I see it as a fortuitous by-product of both of our personalities.

At my 50th I had about 70 guests, people I'd picked up over half a century, most of whom are coming again tonight. Because they have now served an extra ten-year term as friends, they are dearer to me than before. But now, at the 11th hour, and just in time for my 60th birthday, my friendship group has broadened to include my new teacher friends, most of whom are less than half my age and look indistinguishable from my children. As I have renounced worry for the night, I am trying not to fret about how the teachers will respond to the size of my house or how they will get on with the former editor of the *FT*. Kwame, my favourite maths teacher, already calls me the Queen because of the high-handed way I deal with my superiors at school. Now, on surveying the house and the garden slack-jawed, he declares it to be, fittingly, a palace. I'm cringing slightly, but I think it's OK. As the evening unfolds I note one of the teachers is flirting with Stan – which is weird but mainly quite funny. In the corner is my mentor, Marcel, in earnest conversation with my friend Kathryn's new husband, who is a bishop. Both seem perfectly happy.

I dance with my children and with my old and new friends to 'Billie Jean' (which the young think is daringly un-PC). We dance to 'Boogie Wonderland' and 'Stayin' Alive' and to assorted anthems of my youth, assembled into a playlist by Maud. It is 2.30am by the time I get to bed, a full five hours past my usual bedtime.

Around dawn I stumble to the bathroom to get some water. There I notice something odd – long black rubber marks on the bottom of the bath and an empty Prosecco bottle by the side of it. On Monday back at school the mystery is solved: it turns out that two teachers, one in her 20s and the other a Now Teach trainee in her early 60s, had taken themselves on a tour of the house, liked the look of the bath and got into it fully dressed, one at each end, and proceeded to drink and chat riotously. This, I decide, is the sign of a great party.

I did not expect 60 to be like this. I don't think it can have been what the Mayor of London expected either when he judged me to be so doddery he allowed me to get a free bus pass. Everything seems upside down: in no time at all, when I'm 62, I will draw my *FT* pension, to which I started contributing nearly 40 years earlier. Back then, when I looked at my first payslip and saw money taken off for the impossibly distant eventuality of retirement, I felt pensions were a swindle – surely I'd be dead by then.

Instead of being dead, an astonishing thing has happened. In some ways my life has more in common with the 20-somethings at my party than with some of my friends, as I'm at the start, professionally and possibly romantically, and am as silly as they are. The thought of going to a party and sitting in a bath fully dressed drinking heavily with a 25-year-old makes perfect sense to me.

So what is 60: is it old or is it not? I'm as muddled about my age as I was when I was an adolescent. When I was 14, I'd spend Saturday mornings in my bedroom arranging and rearranging my tin of felt-tip pens in order of colour, and then in the evenings I would go to the Freemasons Arms in Hampstead and get drunk on lager-and-lime. Now the confusion is even greater. Despite the fact I'm just starting out in a new job and going on dates, my Google history tells a different story with its searches for exercises for stiff hips and for the best remedies for water-lily beetle. My bank records reveal that alongside payments of the odd tenner to eBay for patent-leather ankle boots, the single biggest expenditure (apart from periodic payments to builders to fix endless leaks in the house) is to my dentist for root canals and dental implants. If teeth are the surest way of judging the age of a body, my broken tusks show me to be very old indeed.

*

One of the difficulties with this new phase of life is that we don't have the vocabulary for it. When I tell people I'm happy about reaching this milestone they mostly reply with brave jocularity: 'Life begins at 60!' or '60 is just a number!' I'm not sure which annoys me most. Life does not begin at 60; by definition it has been going on for an inordinately long time already. And the idea that 60 could be 'just' a number not only offends the maths teacher in me but is plain wrong.

Sixty years is an exact measurement of how long I have been alive; like everyone born in the UK in 1959 I can name Babs from Pan's People, I remember the excitement of the first *Monty Python* episodes, I did my homework by candlelight during the coal strikes, and I know how to address an envelope. These things are fundamental to the person I am now. The reason people produce these dud aphorisms is they are frightened of being 60 and are vainly trying to make it sound better.

I recently read *Extra Time* by Camilla Cavendish in which she points out that living longer doesn't mean an interminable old age, but that middle age lasts a lot longer than it used to. She makes a suggestion – which I like a lot – that instead of measuring our age by how many years we have lived already, we think in terms of how many we have left. This sounds banal but the shift in perspective is oddly profound.

Clearly this is unknowable; as my sister Kate likes to warn me, I could drop down dead at any time. She's right, but so what? The very worst advice I've ever heard is to live every day as if it were the last – if I did that, it would lead to poor, short-term decisions, to telling my children I love them far more often than they have the stomach for, and to morbidity and depression. Instead I now live each day on the assumption that there are tens of thousands more where that one came from. Even if this turns out not to be the case, it seems the sanest thing to do.

In any event, I have the actuaries on my side. I consulted an online life-expectancy calculator and answered a series of questions (mostly honestly, though I did shave a little off my alcohol consumption), and almost instantaneously the computer returned an age of 93. 'Great job!' was the verdict, which was baffling as I wasn't aware of having done any job on this at all. Then I asked Aviva, which gave more or less the same answer.

Because this remaining slice – 33 years in my case – is so long, gerontologists have started cutting it in two. The first slice they call 'young-old', which runs from 60 to about 75 and covers the period when you are healthy and can still do most things – presumably including becoming a teacher and going on dates. 'Young-old' is followed by 'old-old', which is not so jolly and when, by the same argument, you are not so likely to be going on dates and starting new careers. I don't want to think about that period now. I am doing with 'old-old' what I used to do with 'old' in my mind – I am refusing to countenance it.

I'm pleased with this new subdivision and I like the sound of 'young-old', as its pair of opposite adjectives describes the state of my mind and body perfectly. More than that, I'm pleased with my experience of it. So far, I'm finding young-old is much more enjoyable than young-young, which I remember as stressful and intense rather than the great fun it's cracked up to be. My 20s were a decade of inadequacy: worrying about whether I was good enough, cool enough, attractive enough and successful enough. I look at my stressed young colleagues, weighed down by the need to get their lives on track, to get promoted and to prove themselves, and feel carefree by comparison.

One morning I come into work to find one of my teacher friends slumped in her chair in the maths office, groaning.

Serena: I feel like shit . . .

Me: What's the matter?

Serena: I went on a date last night and got so drunk I was sick in the shower this morning.

Me: Blimey. I hope it was fun.

Serena: I can't remember. Why did I have so many drinks? He didn't pay for anything – I spent eighty quid. I can't believe it. (*groans*)

Me: I can't bear a man who is mean.

Serena: Why do I keep going on dates with all these idiots? I've deleted the app. I can't go on doing this.

*

I watch her gather her things for teaching and envy her stamina – she is going to get through a day of lessons just fine. But I don't envy her the rest of it, as the stakes for her are so much higher than they are for me. She is after someone to have children with and set up house with and spend her whole life with. When successive candidates prove entirely unsuitable, her distress grows. In one way I'm in a worse position as far fewer men click 'like' on my profile (and fewer still since the grey hair), but this is a piffling drawback compared to the immeasurable advantage I have of not needing a man anything like as badly as she does.

The following week:

Serena: Did you go on any dates at the weekend?

Me: I went for a walk on Hampstead Heath with a man who didn't ask me a single question.

Serena: How do you get through it without alcohol?!

Me: It's fine. When you're walking you don't have to look at each other – which was just as well as this guy kept stopping to piss behind a tree as he said he had a problem with his prostate.

Her: Gross!!!

Me: Afterwards he sent me a message saying that he didn't feel there was any 'chemistry' between us, but could I help him get his idea for a business promoted in the *FT*?

Her: Fucking cheek. Were you upset?

Me: Not really. I went out and watered my garden.

My friend Emma comes to dinner. She's as young-old as I am, has been divorced for over a decade, and is attractive, funny, high-powered and sane. Whenever I see her we talk about the state of the world, our jobs, our children and – if there is anything to report – whatever dates we've been on.

I tell her that I'm writing this book and that I have been thinking about our stage of life and wondering, in our circumstances, what a man is actually for. The last time we were looking for a match we wanted husbands, fathers to our children, security, someone to buy property with, lifetime companions – all the things Serena wants. We already have children and houses and security and independent lives and neither of us are at all keen on the thought of a man moving in, encroaching.

I tell her about a friend of mine who is a couple of years older than us and who, after a long time dating without noticeable success, has met someone she really likes. When I went round to her house for dinner the other day an outsize silver Buddha with bulging eyes and bell had appeared in her elegant sitting room, alongside the new man who has taken up residence. I'm not sure I'd be up for that.

Emma says she used to think she needed a man for company, but as her adult children perpetually fail to leave home (as do mine) there is little chance of loneliness. Maybe when they finally move out we will feel differently, but even then, if we need to talk to someone we have each other – as well as assorted other friends who have a proven record of providing congenial company, built up over many decades.

After a bit more deliberating we agree that the main purpose of a man to young-old women like us, is intimacy, sex and, possibly, love – though Emma says she's not sure if she's up for the latter anymore.

'Don't think I can suspend disbelief long enough,' she says.

A couple of months later I ring her.

Me: Did you see Guardian Soulmates is closing down?
Emma: I did. Is that going to cramp your style?
Me: No. I'm giving up dating.

I tell her I recently had a drink with a man which I thought went well, though when he asked what I was after, I found myself going through my list of all the things I wasn't looking for in a man. With hindsight, I think he might not have liked that. In any case, a fortnight after the date, I messaged him suggesting another meeting but he said he'd already found someone else.

Emma: Mmm. Maybe better to skip the list next time?
Me: There's not going to be a next time.

Six months later, I'm on the phone to Emma again.

Me: You know that man I told you about?
Emma: Which one?

Me: The one I regaled with all things I didn't want? He got back in touch and we had supper. I think I quite like him.

Emma: Hmm. Keep me posted. Maybe I'll try again too ...

And this, it seems, is the pattern. Sometimes I'm on my own, and sometimes I'm not. When I'm on my own I'm mostly content, working hard and seeing friends and raising marigolds for my garden. But then I start longing for intimacy, and usually find it for a bit, but then the minute I start wondering what a man is for things tend to fall to pieces.

This odd pattern of seasons with men and seasons without rather suits me. Maybe it will continue. Or maybe I'll give up and devote myself wholeheartedly to my children, friends, pupils, garden and house. That would not seem a bad state of affairs. Or maybe I will meet someone I like so much I will overturn my ban on silver Buddhas and allow him – and any dodgy belongings – into my house as well as my life. I don't know, and not knowing is not unsettling at all. It makes the present more interesting.

12

Reinventing Myself

This book is supposed to be about reinvention. I have reinvented great swathes of my life, but have I managed to reinvent myself?

I don't know the answer to this. I don't know the answer in a big philosophical way – are we stuck with the person we happen to be, or can we become someone slightly better? And if so, does that come about by design or by accident? Even less do I know the answer about me in particular. Am I different to what I was like five years ago?

I don't even know who is best placed to judge this. Is it me? Or is it the people who are on the receiving end of me? In some ways I'm the highest authority, but equally I'm too close to the subject to be trusted. So I decide to put the question to people who know me best and let them settle the matter. On a whim, during the weird, thumb-twiddling days of the first coronavirus lockdown, when the school is closed and when I have little else to do, I fire off an email to a panel of 15 – my four children, my sister and my ten closest friends – and ask them point blank.

Dearest best friends and family,

Will you help me?

I'm trying to write a book about reinvention and I'm interested in whether it is possible to change who you are as a result of changing your job. Rather than pontificate on whether I think I've changed as a person now I'm a teacher, I thought I'd ask you instead.

There are seven questions below. All can be simply answered yes/no/don't know, but it would be really great if you could add reasons. Don't hold back. Rose says I must also promise not to ring you to remonstrate. Am happy with that.

1. Am I more self-righteous?
2. Am I less cynical?
3. Have I got any nicer?
4. Am I more interesting?
5. Am I more humourless?
6. Am I more humble?
7. Am I more scary?

Are there any other ways in which I've changed (please specify)?

THANK YOU.

xxxx

*

The hasty, unscientific way I fire off this message is evidence of lack of progress in one important area. I am, it seems, irredeemably careless. I don't bother to consider the etiquette of sending out this solipsistic survey. Least of all do I stop to think how I will feel if they take me at my word and answer honestly.

At the time it seemed a fine idea, and for each of the seven points I could make a good case for some change having taken place. By far the most exciting was the third count – that I've got nicer. This had occurred to me a few days earlier when talking to a former investment banker who'd become a teacher of languages through Now Teach, and who told me he'd become nicer as a result of spending his life with people from different backgrounds and trying to see the world from their point of view.

In that case, I thought, I must be nicer too. I am keen to know if my friends and family agree, but don't want to lead the jury too shamelessly, so I bury the suggestion some way down the list.

I'm also hoping I might have become a bit more humble. I've spent the last three years trying to do something that I'm not naturally good at and watching people half my age doing it much better. Opening yourself to the certainty of failure and swallowing the inevitable humiliation day after day – that has to be character-forming somehow. I think it's also probable that I've become less cynical. The effect of not writing a newspaper column every week and swapping the company of sarky journalists for bright-eyed children must also have had some sort of impact?

On the negative side, I sometimes feel that through my endless proselytising I'm becoming a bit self-righteous. Every time I write anything about teaching, people moan online about virtue-signalling. Equally, I may have become a bit more humourless, as the sort of person who co-founds a worthy education charity is likely to be much less of a laugh than the sort of person who writes comic columns. Possibly scarier too, having practised giving frightening stares which seem to do the trick of silencing classes of 14-year-olds.

I press 'send' on my message and, such is the paucity of things to do during lockdown, answers start to ping back right away. Stella's comes first, barely three minutes after I've sent mine.

> Lucy dear
> I don't think you have changed at all. AT ALL.
> I think all that happens in life is that we shake up our pack of cards (dealt out long long ago) and different ones come to the top. A lot of this has to do with age anyway.

Stella is a writer and her metaphor is just the high-quality thing I would have expected from her. But to extend it a bit further, if we each have 52 cards at birth, isn't there plenty of scope for radical reshuffling? So maybe my cynical card has slipped from the top down to the bottom of the pack, while a hitherto rare humility card that previously never got played is now in constant use? If so, wouldn't that amount to a fairly radical change?

Next comes Maud, my second daughter. She sends the questions back to me, complete with comments.

1. Am I more self-righteous? Yes. This book = point proven. Apparently everyone should teach now.
2. Am I less cynical? No. You were born like that. Sorry.
3. Have I got any nicer? Can't say.
4. Am I more interesting? No, sorry.
5. Am I more humourless? No. Your humour is still lovely.
6. Am I more humble? Is this humble?
7. Am I more scary? Not to me. Your scariness only works on people who don't know you.

Ah well, I think, reading this characteristically sharp, funny reply. I did ask for it.

As more answers come in, themes start to emerge, none particularly to my liking. Only one out of 15 give the responses that I was angling for, concluding I'd become more open-minded, less dismissive and most definitely more humble. Though even she draws the line at saying I've got nicer,

Emma, who is one of my closest but most argumentative friends, is particularly insistent on this point.

> I wouldn't have called you nice in the past, and I wouldn't now. You are an extremely complex bundle of characteristics, most of which I love and some of which I tolerate.

This is an extremely complex bundle of an answer. Pot calls the kettle black, I think.

There is, alas, considerable agreement with Maud in her answer to the first question. About half my survey respondents report some evidence that I've become more self-righteous. Emma feels this particularly strongly, dragging out an incident that occurred shortly after I became a teacher.

> You have developed a tendency to dismiss the troubles of prosperous people. E.g. I remember one time when I was wittering on about the pressures on middle-class children you shut me up by saying that given the extreme pressures the children in your class were under, you didn't have much sympathy with said middle-class kids. Which would be OK if you were writing an article, but I wasn't making a statement about what the government's priorities should be – I was looking for a friendly fat-chewing session about things of interest to me and our friends.

*

I read this and feel unrepentant on that particular occasion but mortified in general. If I have turned into a prig, I resolve to make a conscious effort to reshuffle the pack so that that ugly card returns to the bottom.

Otherwise no one seems to think I've changed much at all, with my sister, Kate, particularly adamant on this front ('No, to all the above'). One or two friends think I might have got a bit less cynical; my friend Marina is unkind enough to point to a particularly sarky article I wrote ten years ago about an all-women charity bike ride the pair of us had been on, and suggests I'd be unlikely to write that now.

In the course of this ill-advised exercise, all sorts of other things come crawling out of the woodwork. Kathryn, who I have walked with every Saturday morning for about two decades, says she's learnt to deal with my scariness by not raising any topics likely to make me cross. My ex-colleague Gideon puts it more bluntly:

I have always found you scary and I continue to do so.
You are a bully, in the nicest possible way.

Apart from the new and regrettable tendency towards self-righteousness, my friends seem to see me roughly as they always did – the new job has made no noticeable difference. They like me no more or less than previously. Some find me slightly more interesting, but that depends on what they are interested in themselves.

Is this good? Is it disappointing? I think it may be both. I like change in general so am vaguely discouraged to discover I have managed to do so very little reshuffling of my own deck of cards. But in a way it is reassuring to think the things that make us who we are remain so strong that they endure despite even the most radical rearrangement of the furniture.

I am pondering this when I get the final response. Jasper has been my friend my entire life. Our parents were Australians together settling into London in the 1950s, and he has known me the longest and the best. Against each of my suggested changes he has typed in emphatic red: NO. At the bottom he has added:

> Any other changes? You are happier. Although I never would have predicted that you would become a teacher, now that you have, it seems very natural – almost obvious. So perhaps the answer is that you haven't changed because what you have done is simply to turn a different part of yourself towards the sun, as it were. It was always there.

This pleases me greatly. I love the idea of having a different part turned towards the sun. His words are lovely, but is he right? I never ask myself if I'm happy, because too much asking leads to dissatisfaction, and because happiness itself is so quixotic. But now he raises the matter, I'd say the first three years of my new life have been happier than the last three of my old one.

I might have left it there, but then I look again at my email and two friends – with time evidently hanging too heavy on them – have messaged again.

'I've had another thought,' writes Madeleine, who, more than any of my other friends, was prepared to think I really might have changed for the better.

> I've noticed it since the teaching began – you are grateful for your friends, your children and your house. It seems to me this gratitude might be a result of you liking yourself more.

I know she means this as a good thing but isn't this evidence of more priggishness? To feel grateful is good, but to bang on about it to your friends is inexcusable. As for liking myself, what does that even mean? I neither like nor dislike myself as a person, because it has never seemed to apply.

The second email is from Stella.

> A couple more thoughts. I suppose other options might be, in a therapist-style way, to put the question to you. Did you ever invent yourself??? If not, how can you reinvent yourself? With a teacher mother and a historian father, isn't the 'reinvention' more along the lines of a poignant return to the family fold?

*

239

This is a slight spanner in the works. If I'm no longer allowed the vulgar concept of reinvention, I wonder what else I can add to my story to make it more than a mundane reversion to type, set long ago by my parents.

The message gets worse.

> It's easier for baby boomers, lucky with property, pensions, etc. to move house or job because we can. To attribute the opportunity to switch careers to individual will is also to buy into an idea of agency that is over-inflated.

So not only have I not reinvented myself but my agency in being able to change was no big deal because I'm so privileged. She's right, but still I'm unrepentant. Even if change was simply returning to the fold, and even if it was easy to do (it wasn't, especially), it still feels quite a big deal to me.

I entirely accept the ruling of my friends and family that I have hopelessly failed to reinvent myself, but inside I still feel different. I now see what should have been obvious all along – what has changed is not my character but my experiences. I am immersed in a new world that feels a long way away from my old one. Though I've not been reinvented, what has happened is just as radical and a lot more interesting: I am being re-educated.